I0089260

Steve Hawke grew up in Melbourne, but found his way to the Northern Territory, and then to the Kimberley, as a 19-year-old in 1978. Captivated by the country, the history and the people, he finished up staying for almost 15 years, working for Aboriginal communities and organisations. He now lives in the hills outside Perth, but continues his strong association with the Kimberley, returning most years. His writings on the Kimberley include *Noonkanbah* (1989); *Barefoot Kids* (2007), a children's novel set in Broome; and *A Town Is Born* (2013), a history of Fitzroy Crossing. He has worked with the Bunuba community for 30 years, on the *Jandamarra* project and other cultural projects for Bunuba Cultural Enterprises, and also on a wide range of community, organisational, land and native title projects and activities.

Conflict in the Bunuba camp in the 2011 BCE production at Windjana Gorge, WA. (Photo: Matt Scurfield)

JANDAMARRA

STEVE HAWKE

Developed from the stories of the Bunuba people,
and from the book
Jandamarra and the Bunuba Resistance
by Howard Pedersen and Banjo Woorunmurra

Bunuba translation by Mona Oscar, Patsy Bedford,
Selina Middleton & June Oscar

Kriol translation by Patsy Bedford, Danny Marr,
June Oscar & Michelle Martin

Dramaturgy by Phil Thomson with Kelton Pell

CURRENCY PLAYS

First published in 2014
by Currency Press Pty Ltd,
PO Box 2287, Strawberry Hills, NSW, 2012, Australia
enquiries@currency.com.au
www.currency.com.au

Copyright: Introduction © June Oscar, 2013; Director's Notes © Phil Thomson, 2014; *Jandamarra* © Bunuba Cultural Enterprises, 2014; photographs © Bunuba Cultural Enterprises

COPYING FOR EDUCATIONAL PURPOSES

The Australian *Copyright Act 1968* (Act) allows a maximum of one chapter or 10% of this book, whichever is the greater, to be copied by any educational institution for its educational purposes provided that that educational institution (or the body that administers it) has given a remuneration notice to Copyright Agency Limited (CAL) under the Act. For details of the CAL licence for educational institutions contact CAL, Level 15/233 Castlereagh Street, Sydney, NSW, 2000; tel: within Australia 1800 066 844 toll free; outside Australia 61 2 9394 7600; fax: 61 2 9394 7601; email: info@copyright.com.au

COPYING FOR OTHER PURPOSES

Except as permitted under the Act, for example a fair dealing for the purposes of study, research, criticism or review, no part of this book may be reproduced, stored in a retrieval system, or transmitted in any form or by any means without prior written permission. All enquiries should be made to the publisher at the address above.

Any performance or public reading of *Jandamarra* is forbidden unless a licence has been received from the author or the author's agent. The purchase of this book in no way gives the purchaser the right to perform the play in public, whether by means of a staged production or a reading. All applications for public performance should be addressed to Bunuba Cultural Enterprises, PO Box 200, Mundaring, WA 6073; email info@jandamarra.com.au

Cataloguing-in-Publication data for this title is available from the National Library of Australia website, www.nla.gov.au.

Typeset by Dean Nottle for Currency Press.
Cover design by Emma Vine.

Front cover shows the full cast dancing the Yilimbirri Junba. Back cover shows (left to right) Sandra Umbagai-Clarke as Mayannie, Kelton Pell as Marralam, Damion Hunter as Jandamarra and Emmanuel Brown as Yilimarra. Both photographs are from the 22 July 2011 Bunuba Cultural Enterprises production at Windjana Gorge. Photographer: Matt Scur ield.

Currency Press acknowledges the Traditional Owners of the Country on which we live and work. We pay our respects to all Aboriginal and Torres Strait Islander Elders, past and present.

Contents

Introduction
  June Oscar   *vii*

Director's Notes
  Phil Thomson   *xiii*

JA<u>N</u>DAMARRA

  Act One   1

  Act Two   43

The full cast dance the Yilimbirri Junba to close the show in the 2011 BCE production at Windjana Gorge, WA. (Photo: Matt Scurfield)

INTRODUCTION

I am a Bunuba woman from Fitzroy Crossing, in the Kimberley region of Western Australia. As a young woman in the 1980s I began working with Bunuba Productions, a company established by my elders with the aim of bringing the story of Jandamarra to the world as a feature film.

It is the story of a young man shot down near Tunnel Creek in 1897 by a police tracker at the age of just 24. For the three years before this he had led one of the most prolonged and successful campaigns of Indigenous resistance in the history of the Australian frontier. This was after he had spent time as a police tracker, hunting and imprisoning his own people, until the fateful night he shot his friend, trooper Richardson, and rejoined the Bunuba.

The resistance began with a major pitched battle at Bandilngan—Windjana Gorge—in which he was grievously wounded. Whilst he hovered near death in Tunnel Creek, hundreds upon hundreds of Indigenous people were killed in reprisal and hunting raids led by the police. When Jandamarra recovered he adopted guerrilla tactics that kept the pastoralists at bay, and allowed his people to continue to live in the northern part of Bunuba Country. The rugged nature of our country, with its limestone ranges riddled with secret caves and springs, provided him and us with refuge.*

But there are other elements of his story, beyond the history of killings and conflict, of land as territory to be won or lost, that have lived on around Bunuba campfires, from the 1890s until today, in stories, and song, and dance.

Jandamarra became a Jalgangurru, a man of magical and mystical powers. He could escape his pursuers by transforming into a bird. And as a Jalgangurru, he took on the responsibility of defending not only the land, but the spirits and powers that give the land life and meaning.

* For a full account of the history, see *Jandamarra and the Bunuba Resistance* by Howard Pedersen in collaboration with Bunuba elder Banjo Woorunmurra (Magabala Press).

These matters lie at the heart of our telling of the Jandamarra story, and of the film we hoped to make.

For more than 20 years we pursued this dream, at times coming agonisingly close. Then in 2004 a new possibility emerged: Tom Gutteridge of the Perth-based Black Swan State Theatre Company spoke with our writer Steve Hawke about the idea of adapting our unproduced film script as a stage play.

This idea became a reality with the premiere, sellout season of *Jandamarra* at the Perth International Arts Festival in February 2008 as a co-production between Black Swan and our company, Bunuba Cultural Enterprises.

The process of developing this new production was an exciting and stimulating time for the Bunuba community. We were able to explore and develop the themes of law, religion and spirituality that are the core of the story for us. We were able to imagine the motivations and context for critical moments such as the shooting of Richardson in a way that rang true to the Bunuba world view. We found a way to incorporate the Yilimbirri Junba—a song and dance cycle dreamed by one of our late elders, Adam Andrews, that reflects the Jandamarra story—as a central element of the play, with senior elder George Brooking as the singer.

Three of our community members, Danny Marr, Emmanuel Brown and Kevin Spratt, emerged through a workshop process to take roles in the cast and make their acting debuts. Young artist Kaylene Marr worked with designer Zoe Atkinson to create beautiful animations representing the Bunuba spiritual world that became a highlight of the production.

A key moment was the decision made during the first reading of the script that we would render those scenes set in the Bunuba world in the Bunuba language on stage. This led to myself, my mother Mona Oscar, and my sisters Patsy Bedford and Selina Middleton working with Steve to translate a third of his original text.

I grew up speaking my language, and speak it still to this day. I served for many years as the chairperson of the Kimberley Language Resource Centre, an organisation devoted to promoting and protecting our Indigenous languages. I am passionate about the role of language as a central part of our being and our identity as proud Indigenous people.

The opportunity to use our language and interpreting skills in such a new and dynamic way was a joy to my mother, my sisters and I. The process gave the play a whole new life and meaning for us. We were able to contribute to the dramatic development and the truthfulness of the play and the world it was portraying, as well as the language. We then had to teach an Indigenous cast drawn from all over Australia not just to talk Bunuba, but to think and to be Bunuba on stage. They embraced this challenge magnificently.

For Patsy and I the two months of rehearsal and performance in early 2008, where we worked as language coaches and cultural advisers was a truly magical time of creativity and pride. Becoming involved in the world of theatre was a new and rich experience. It was thrilling to bring an Indigenous language—our language, Bunuba—in all its complexity and richness, to the Australian main stage.

The production was a true collaboration between highly skilled theatre practitioners, and artists and cultural leaders from a traditional Indigenous community. For the Bunuba community it was an entirely positive experience. My mother cried tears of joy and pride when she flew down for opening night. We thank Black Swan for their willingness to embrace and implement such an approach.

For all the joy of that initial production, there was one major disappointment. For budgetary reasons, it was just impossible for us to mount the show in the Kimberley for our home audience. From the day the first season ended, we began work on plans to mount a Kimberley tour. Black Swan was not in a position to be involved in such a tour, so the project became an independent initiative of Bunuba Cultural Enterprises. It took us three and a half years, but we got there.

Very early in the piece we brought Phil Thomson on board as the new director and dramaturg. It proved to be an inspired choice. His natural insight and energy, backed by his long experience working on Indigenous projects and with Indigenous actors, was the perfect fit for a project that was challenging in artistic, production and budgetary terms.

The script was extensively reworked for the new production. By the time we were ready to go, there was a considerable turnover in the cast. Damion Hunter replaced Jimi Bani in the lead role, and did so with distinction. Danny Marr reprised his role as the elder Dibinarra. But our two younger locals, Emmanuel Brown and Kevin Spratt, both stepped up to more significant roles; Emmanuel from Ilaji to the warrior leader Yilimarra, and Kevin from Darrudi to replace Emmanuel as Ilaji.

We thought we had a crisis on our hands when Kimberley stalwart Ningali Lawford-Wolf was unavailable to play the important role of Jini, mother of Jandamarra. But then Patsy Bedford stepped into the breach. Phil put her to a stern test in auditions, but she came through with flying colours, to make her stage debut as a 60-year-old. Having Patsy, as a senior Bunuba leader and a fluent language speaker, up there on stage lent a whole new feel to the show, and the Kimberley audiences loved her.

We believe that the Jandamarra Returns tour of the Kimberley in July–August 2011 was a significant achievement, and something of a milestone in Australian theatre.

As a small, remote, Indigenous company we were able to raise a budget of $1.14 million, excluding development costs, and mount a tour in some of the most challenging and remote country in Australia, and even return a tiny profit. Our heartfelt thanks are due to the funding agencies and sponsors too numerous to mention here.

We put on a fully professional show of the highest production values at four outdoor venues, created from scratch. School ovals in Broome and Kununurra. A free community performance at the foot of Red Hill in Lundja Community on the outskirts of Halls Creek. And the highlight season: five nights at Windjana Gorge, 140 kilometres from the nearest town, in the heart of Bunuba Country, and a key location in the historical story.

We averaged houses of 400 a night over the tour. Through a community access ticketing program we were able to ensure that the local Indigenous communities got to the show. For many, if not the majority, it was their first experience of professional theatre. At venue after venue, old people in particular were reduced to tears by seeing their history and heritage portrayed with such vibrancy and authenticity.

And having the chance to rework and reshape the show was a blessing. There is no doubt that second time around it was a stronger, more polished and more powerful piece of theatre. Novelist Gail Jones wrote in *The Monthly* after seeing the show at Windjana Gorge, 'We can't really speak when the production finishes. There is the shyness, the reserve, that true artworks inspire.'

Our most important audience was the Bunuba community. On the last day of the tour Patsy Bedford reflected on this:

> It was really spiritual for us. We knew the place had come alive. We had brought the place alive although Jandamarra is gone, but we think Jandamarra is still alive now, more alive in a different way. Bunuba people have got more strength to fight in different ways for what we want in this day. As Bunuba People, we're fighters in our own right in the Western world with politics, and whatever's going on with our land, our language, and our culture, and I think this has made us stronger for our tomorrow.

Our tomorrow is about much more than just making theatre. The Bunuba community is engaged with the modern world as pastoralists and entrepreneurs, as conservationists and land managers, and as educational innovators. With the other peoples of the Fitzroy Valley we are actively working on programs to combat the scourge of alcoholism and the terrible effects of Foetal Alcohol Spectrum Disorders, and to rebuild and strengthen family life in our communities.

But all of this will amount to little if we do not hold strong to our culture and our history. The *Jandamarra* play has been vitally important in this regard to our community, as well as being great fun. It is also something that we have been able to offer to the world beyond our small, remote township of Fitzroy Crossing.

Jandamarra is a big, expensive show. So far we have not been able to secure any further tours or productions; but we are persistent and patient. And we will continue to work on new ways of bringing the Jandamarra story, and Bunuba language and culture to audiences in Australia and beyond. The experience has enabled us to broaden our vision and embrace new directions. We are currently working with composer Paul Stanhope, and the Sydney Symphony Orchestra and Gondwana Choirs, to develop a new cantata for performance at the Sydney Opera House in 2014, with a number of the performers from the play, and the singers and dancers from the Yilimbirri Junba ensemble. We are developing new theatre projects: in Indigenous languages for Kimberley schools, and mainstream projects for some of the local actors who emerged through the two seasons of *Jandamarra*.

I have been involved in the *Jandamarra* project virtually all of my adult life. I am immensely proud of what we have achieved over the two seasons of the play.

Jandamarra lives on.

Bunuba language and culture stand strong.

June Oscar
January 2013

June Oscar is a Company Director of Bunuba Cultural Enterprises. She worked as a linguist, language coach and cultural adviser on both the 2008 and 2011 productions of *Jandamarra*.

Sandra Umbagai-Clarke as Mayannie, Kelton Pell as Marralam and Steve Turner as Joe in the 2011 BCE production at Windjana Gorge, WA. (Photo: Matt Scurfield)

DIRECTOR'S NOTES

When I had the privilege to be asked to direct 'Jandamarra Returns' I agreed on the proviso that I also work as dramaturge with writer Steve Hawke to help him evolve his original work into a more dynamic and immediate telling of this magnificent story.

From the beginning I saw the similarities between this story and classic Greek tragedy. There is the interplay between gods (the Ungguds) and mortals, and Jandamarra's fateful journey is reminiscent of those of the Greek heroes. This recognition informed Steve Hawke's rewriting of the work, allowing us to create a classic structure and suggesting a powerful acting style that would communicate across the great outdoor venues we were to inhabit.

One of the strengths of Indigenous performance is its inclusion of the audience in the telling. The original script was a 'memory play' in which two older characters shared memories of the bad times, with the unfortunate consequence of ignoring the audience. In rewriting we chose to allow characters to speak directly to their listeners, sharing feelings and insights directly from a chain gang or the heat of battle. This proved to be a powerful device.

It was also important to me that we played the action, rather than describe it. Designer Bryan Woltjen created an evocative structural set on which the cast could run, battle, leap and dance. Staging the gun battles with loud gunshots and athletic deaths created a spectacle that enthralled even the 12-year-old boys in the audience. The evocative, non-natural lighting by Joe Mecurio added to the other-worldly, epic nature of the production, as did David Pye's awesome sound score. When these elements were added to Kaylene Marr's naïve Bunuba animations we created magic under the stars.

The play is written in English, Bunuba and Kriol (the Kimberley version of Pidgin English), giving the work great veracity and the opportunity for audiences to experience the depth and sophistication of traditional language. However I was concerned by the idea of sur-titling all of the non-English scenes... this has a great danger of lifting the audience's eye from the action to read the show in English rather than listening to the Bunuba. Instead we only sur-titled key lines and questions, allowing the audience to understand what a scene was about but forcing them to listen to tone and watch body language to become fully immersed in the drama. When we did use projected translations I instructed the actors to breathe-in the ramifications of those key lines, giving a pause in the action so the audience missed nothing. This proved to be a highly successful solution to a major problem of mixed language productions.

By casting Bunuba performers alongside professional actors from across Australia we were able to incorporate authentic language, dance, song and spirit within the framework of a Western play. The experienced actors shared their skills to lift the performances of the newcomers, and the Bunuba mob passed on the deeply spiritual and political aspects of the work. It was a brilliant mix of performers and cultures.

The real key to the success of the play was, however, the immense trust given to we foreign theatre-makers by the traditional owners of the story. They led us into secret caves, shared deep culture, and allowed us to play with their significant stories. They gave us creative freedom, but guided and instructed us with strength when we took it too far. The Bunuba believe Jandamarra still lives, his spirit still guiding them, and they have chosen to embrace theatre and other artforms to share his story with the world. This willingness to share and to use artforms from non-Bunuba cultures is most inspiring... I believe it is the best way for humans to understand and relate maturely to one another. Artists have a much deeper role than that of mere entertainers... they enable and ennoble us.

Being beneath the cliffs of Windjana Gorge as mix-raced audiences became immersed in this extraordinary tale of courage, magic, massacre and redemption was perhaps the most powerful theatre experience of my life. I am so thankful to have been given the chance to be involved, and to all of the army of technicians, riggers, managers, designers, performers, language and cultural coaches, singers, actors and elders who travelled the Kimberley together.

And many thanks to writer Steve Hawke who trusted me to direct his work, and who accepted my criticisms and crazy ideas with such an open mind. He produced this epic event and wrote a play that I believe will be performed as a classic in years to come. That Jandamarra lives again with such vigor has much to do with Steve's sacrifice, tenacity and collaborative spirit. Thanks mate.

Phil Thomson
June 2014

Margaret Mills as Mary, Steve Turner as Joe, Damion Hunter as Jandamarra and Trevor Ryan as Mingo Mick in the 2011 BCE production at Windjana Gorge, WA. (Photo: Matt Scurfield)

Jandamarra was first produced as a co-production between Black Swan State Theatre Company and Bunuba Cultural Enterprises for the Perth International Arts Festival at Perth Convention Exhibition Centre, on 9 February 2008, with the following cast:

JANDAMARRA	Jimi Bani
YILIMARRA / JACKY	Tony Briggs
SINGER	George Brooking
ILAJI	Emmanuel Brown
LINDSAY / RICHARDSON	Simon Clarke
FORREST	Peter Docker
JOE BLIGH	Geoff Kelso
JINI	Ningali Lawford-Wolf
DIBINARRA	Danny Marr
MARY BLIGH	Margaret Mills
MARRALAM	Kelton Pell
MINGO MICK	Dennis Simmons
DARRUDI / GEORGIE	Kevin Spratt
MAYANNIE / WIYALA	Sandra Umbagai-Clarke

Director, Tom Gutteridge
Associate Director, Ningali Lawford-Wolf
Bunuba Translators, June Oscar, Patsy Bedford, Mona Oscar, Selina Middleton
Language Coaches, June Oscar, Patsy Bedford, Mona Oscar
Cultural Advisers, June Oscar, Patsy Bedford, Mona Oscar, George Brooking
Set & Costume Designer, Zoe Atkinson
Musical Director, Paul Kelly
Lighting Designer, Andrew Lake
Animation Artist, Kaylene Marr
Animator, Clancie Shorter

The play was then revised and rewritten for the 2011 'Jandamarra Returns' Kimberley tour to Broome, Windjana Gorge, Halls Creek and Kununurra. This version was first performed by Bunuba Cultural Enterprises at the Saint Mary's College Oval in Broome, Western Australia, on 13 July 2011, with the following cast:

JANDAMARRA	Damion Hunter
SINGER / WANGAMARRA	Kristin Andrews
JINI	Patsy Bedford
YILIMARRA / JACKY	Emmanuel Brown
DARRUDI / GEORGIE	Mark Coles Smith
RICHARDSON / FORREST	Peter Docker
LINDSAY	Cody Fern
DIBINARRA	Danny Marr
MARY BLIGH	Margaret Mills
MARRALAM	Kelton Pell
MINGO MICK	Trevor Ryan
ILAJI	Kevin Spratt
JOE BLIGH	Steve Turner
MAYANNIE / WIYALA	Sandra Umbagai-Clarke

Director & Dramaturge, Phil Thomson
Associate Director, Kelton Pell
Bunuba Translators, Language Coaches & Cultural Advisers,
    June Oscar, Patsy Bedford, Mona Oscar
Cultural Adviser—Yilimbirri Junba, Dillon Andrews
Set & Costume Designer, Bryan Woltjen
Sound Designer, David Pye
Lighting Designer, Jo Mercurio
Animation Artist, Kaylene Marr
Animator, Ian Tregonning
AV Design, Mia Holten
Production Manager, Andrew Portwine

Bunuba prisoners are led off to gaol in the 2011 BCE production at Windjana Gorge, WA. (Photo: Matt Scurfield)

AUTHOR'S NOTE

The premiere season of *Jandamarra* was a co-production between the Black Swan State Theatre Company and Bunuba Cultural Enterprises (BCE), presented to sellout houses at the 2008 Perth International Arts Festival. BCE, the owner and copyright holder of the play, is a company owned by the Bunuba people of the Kimberley. They are the custodians of the Jandamarra story.

The funds were not available to take the original production to the Kimberley. BCE felt a strong cultural obligation to take this iconic Kimberley story 'home'.

It took three years of planning and fundraising to realise this dream. In July–August of 2011, BCE mounted the Jandamarra Returns tour, presenting 13 performances at four Kimberley venues; Broome, Halls Creek, Kununurra, and the feature season at Bandilngan—Windjana Gorge—in the heart of Bunuba country, where some of the critical scenes in the play are set, and where many of the historical events took place.

The 2011 season was in effect a new production, with an extensive rewrite, and many new members in the creative team.

This script is the production version, with animation/projection details included, and surtitle notations.

Further information on the production and the Jandamarra Returns tour can be found at the BCE website: www.jandamarra.com.au

SH

NOTES ON LANGUAGE

Jandamarra portrays four distinct linguistic worlds:
- the Bunuba people in their own camps, speaking the Bunuba language;
- the white pastoralists and police, talking English amongst themselves;
- the overlap, where Bunuba people and whites talk to each other in Pidgin English;
- the other overlap, where Bunuba people talk to other Aboriginal people who are non-Bunuba speakers in Kriol, which is a complex language in its own right, quite distinct from Pidgin.

Those scenes, and parts of scenes, in which Bunuba and Kriol are the appropriate languages have been translated from the original English version. The scenes between white and Aboriginal characters have been left in English.

Bunuba Translations

The original translation work was done in Fitzroy Crossing in August and December 2006, and August 2007. The writer worked with Mona Oscar, Patsy Bedford, June Oscar and Selina Middleton. Mona is a Bunuba elder with experience in translation and interpreting work. Patsy, June and Selina are Bunuba women who are all literate in the language. The orthography and spelling system was developed by the Bunuba people, working with the Kimberley Language Resource Centre.

The writer is indebted beyond words to these dedicated and highly skilled women. The task involved much more than straightforward translation. The process can never be exact, as the vocabularies of the two languages only partially overlap, and each contains concepts and implied attitudes which are not shared by the other. The original English version contained language and metaphors that simply did not translate into Bunuba, and at times the writer's imagination of the traditional Bunuba world was lacking, or simply wrong. We were able to work together to find new ways to convey the information and emotion necessary for the drama in a form true to the Bunuba world view. As such, the work was dramaturgy as much as translation; an exciting and intellectually stimulating challenge.

The English translation of the Bunuba components of this script are 'back translations' of the agreed Bunuba version. In many cases the result is something quite distinct from the original English. The outcome is an English version which is much more closely reflective of a Bunuba sensibility than the writer could possibly have achieved on his own.

Kriol Translations

The Kriol translation was a more straightfoward process, but equally important in terms of creating a world that rings true to the people of the Kimberley. Kriol is widely spoken across northern Australia, with many regional variations. Initial translations were done with Patsy Bedford, Danny Marr and June Oscar. Michelle Martin assisted with the orthography and spelling, using the authorised Kimberley version.

Steve Hawke
August 2007

A NOTE ON THE TRANSLATION

For the 2011 production new translations and amendments as required were done with Mona Oscar, June Oscar and Patsy Bedford.

A decision was made for 2011 to not fully surtitle the Bunuba elements. It was felt that this would enable the audience to more fully engage with the action and emotion on stage.

This production script identifies the surtitled elements in bold type.

Bunuba Orthography & Pronunciation

Vowels

a	like the **u** in b**u**t	**aa**	like the **a** in f**a**ther
i	like the **i** in p**i**t	**u**	like the **u** in p**u**t and the **oo** in foot

Consonants

b	as in English	**d**	as in English
d̲	like rd or rt in card, cart	**g**	as in English
j	as inEnglish	**l**	as in English
l̲	like **rl** in gi**rl**	**lh**	no equivalent; place tip of tongue between teeth and make an **l** sound
ly	like the **lli** in mi**lli**on	**m**	as in English
n	as in English	**n̲**	like the **rn** in ba**rn**
ng	as in sing	**nh**	no equivalent; place tip of tongue between teeth and make an **n** sound
ny	like the **ni** in o**ni**on	**r**	as in English
rr	like the rolled Scottish **r**	**th**	soft like the **th** in **th**at
w	as in English	**y**	as in English

Kimberley Kriol Orthography & Pronounciation

Vowels

a	as in man	**ai**	as in rain	**ar**	as in card
e	as in egg	**ee**	as in feet	**i**	as in pit
ie	as in pie	**ir**	as in bird	**o**	as in orange
oa	as in road	**oi**	as in boy	**oo**	as in pool
or	as in horse	**ou**	as in house	**u**	as in cup

Consonants

b for English **b** and **p**   d   for English **d** and **t**

g for English **g**, **k**, **hard c**, **ck**   **rr** like the rolled Scottish **r**

Others as in English

PRINCIPAL CHARACTERS

THE BUNUBA

JANDAMARRA, a Bunuba man, born about 1873

JINI, Jandamarra's mother

DIBINARRA, an elder and lawman, Jandamarra's spiritual mentor

YILIMARRA, Jandamarra's uncle, a leader amongst the Bunuba

MARRALAM, a strong traditionalist, initially antagonistic to Jandamarra

ILAJI, Jandamarra's slightly older cousin

DARRUDI, also Jandamarra's cousin, the same age; youthful playmate

MAYANNIE, lover of Bill Richardson, and then Jandamarra

THE WHITES

JOE BLIGH, the first settler to start a station on Bunuba country, at Lillimooloora

MARY BLIGH, wife of Joe

LINDSAY BLIGH, son of Joe and Mary, 14 years old when the story begins

ALEXANDER FORREST, Kimberley pioneer, Member of Parliament, and business partner of Joe

RICHARDSON, a loner, becomes manager of Lillimooloora, then a policeman

THE TRACKER

MINGO MICK, a Pilbara mabarn (magic man) and tracker

MINOR CHARACTERS

WANGAMARRA, the singer
TROOPER, Constable McDonald
YILIMBIRRI UNGGUD, the snake
BUNUBA MAN
TRACKER
WIYALA, Marralam's wife
GEORGIE, an Aboriginal stockman
JACKY, Mayannie's father
JIM CROWE, an Aboriginal tracker
ALF BARNETT, a trooper
TROOPERS
WARRIORS
PRISONER

SETTING

The action of the play takes place in the West Kimberley region of
Western Australia, primarily at Derby, Lillimooloora Station (Limalurru
to the Bunuba), Bandilngan (Windjana Gorge) and in traditional Bunuba
Country. It begins when Jandamarra is 12 years old, and spans the time
until his death 12 years later, in 1897.

Peter Docker as Richardson and Damion Hunter as Jandamarra at
Bululu in the 2011 BCE production at Windjana Gorge, WA.
(Photo: Matt Scurfield)

ACT ONE

PROLOGUE

The Indigenous actors begin to inhabit the stage, dressed in traditional costume, going about their everyday business.

On cue, the house lights and music go down.

DIBINARRA *moves to the high point, then indicates for silence.*

These first lines are surtitled to set up a convention to be used later.

DIBINARRA: **Winyi wunggurragi. Ngirri.inga mathawirrinyagu thangani Jandamarra.wu, Bunuba.nhi muwayi.** [*Listen up, everybody. We are here to tell you a story about Jandamarra, from Bunuba country.*]

> *He rejoins the Bunuba camp. The rasping of spears being sharpened. Domestic scenes.*
>
> *Projected animation #1: Snake breathing slowly. Peaceful and powerful.*
>
> *Singing and transformation music as the cast enter into the body and spirit of their characters.*

ILAJI: [*offstage*] Yackaaiiii. **Wadgurragaliii Limalurruyawu!** [*They're coming into Limalurru.*]

> ILAJI, JANDAMARRA *and* DARRUDI *charge onto stage. Excited talk and gestures.*
>
> *The* BUNUBA MOB *spread out to hide and watch as:*
>
> MARY, JOE *and* LINDSAY *enter, carrying goods and guns, as a long, exciting day draws to a close.*
>
> MARY *sees smoke in the distance. She calls* JOE *over and points. He indicates that she shouldn't worry.*
>
> *Lights focus on the* BUNUBA. JINI *and* YILIMARRA *call the group together.*

JINI: **Malngarri yani bagawurragi Limalurru yuwa, ngaanyi**

barrma birranggu? [*What are we going to do about these whitefellers camped at Limalurru?*]

YILIMARRA: Malngarri yani ganbawuwirragi nyirraji rarrgi ngilamungga. [*They're all chasing that gold, way to the east.*]

JINI: [*angrily*] Ngayi ngilamungga wadgurragi. [*No, this lot aren't going east.*]

MARRALAM: Ngindaji mindija gimma Yilimarra. [*She's right, Yilimarra.*]

JINI *nods approvingly, as all but* MARRALAM *withdraw from sight.* MARRALAM *talks directly to the audience before joining them.*

Jini was right. This malngarri mob weren't travelling through our country looking for gold. They were moving in to Limalurru. They were here to stay.

SCENE ONE

Evening sounds of birds. Lights pick out JANDAMARRA *and* DARRUDI *watching the* BLIGHS.

LINDSAY *is almost sleepwalking as he accepts a goodnight kiss from* MARY, *then steps down.*

JOE: He'll sleep well.

MARY: He sure will. What a day.

JOE *gives her a hug. She looks back to the ranges.*

That smoke was from campfires, wasn't it?

JOE: Yeah, but they're miles away.

MARY: Are you sure we don't need to set up a watch?

JOE: The dogs'll wake us if there's any trouble.

MARY: I'll take first stint.

JOE: Remember, darling. Show no fear.

She lets him lead her off. Darkness.

Light on the singer, WANGAMARRA, *sitting to the side of the stage at a fire, dressed as a traditional man. He begins to sing:*

WANGAMARRA: [*sung*] Limalurru dawulma bingirri
            Limalurru dawulma bingirri
            Galanganyja dawulma bingirri
            Galanganyja dawulma bingirri

As the song fades, JINI *turns to the audience.*

JINI: My little brother Gumbayi is singing his song. We still dance it today; a song for my son, Jandamarra. For him and Yilimbirri Unggud. The snake and the man, connected together. It all started when he was just a kid, and he chased that white boy Lindsay Bligh, chased his mate all the way to Yilimbirri's spring, trying to stop him. Those malngarri, they were the first lot of white people to sit down in our country, the Bligh mob.

The song fades back up for a few lines.

SCENE TWO

Morning sounds. JANDAMARRA *is still watching from the ranges.*

JOE *and* MARY *enter.*

MARY: So different in the morning light! It's beautiful, Joe. But… a little forbidding.

JOE: The Barrier Range. No-one's been through to the other side yet, but there's sure to be more good country through there. But first, my dear, we'll put our stamp on what we've got. There'll be springs and creeks all along this range. Let's just pray they'll still be running come November.

MARY: Where's Lindsay got to?

JOE: Bringing in the horses. [*Proudly*] Only man I've ever known to beat me out of the swag of a morning.

MARY: He's fourteen, Joe. A boy still. Don't forget that.

LINDSAY: [*charging on*] Dad! Dad, Rhino broke his hobbles and I had to follow him past the spur to the next valley.

MARY: You what?!

LINDSAY: He found the sweetest patch of ribbon grass. It'd be perfect for a horse paddock. You should come and see!

JOE: [*smiling broadly*] There's things to do round here first. Maybe tomorrow, hey son. Come on, you two. Let's get stuck in.

All the BUNUBA *enter, arguing, as the* BLIGHS *exit in high spirits.*

YILIMARRA: Winyiya thangani. **Dangajgawarrinya, limba wadbayali thawunujangi.** [*You've heard the stories. **We kill them, and the police will be swarming like ants.***]

MARRALAM: Wigawuwaduragi. Yaninja wadgurragi. [*We'll just hunt them out then.*]

DIBINARRA: **Nguja yarri.ingga ngayi milu gamanbarra. Wilawarrma nyanangarri.** [*We can't start a fight without talking to the other clans.*]

YILIMARRA: Wad'barrau birriga, winami-yawu, Miluwindiyawu. Milawarra nyirraji nhi. [*Let's go north, to the high ranges. We'll watch them from there.*]

JINI: **Ngindaji Jandamarrau muwayi. Yathawarra ngindaji yuwa.** [*This is Jandamarra's country. We will stay here!*]

YILIMARRA: Yuwayi. Nhir ngawungu guju bagara rawurra. [*True. His father's bones are up there.*] [*To* JINI] Jandamarra-way yathawunggurrantha winyiunggurrantha ngaanyi wilalawurragi. [*You and Jandamarra stay here, listen out for what they are saying.*]

DIBINARRA: **Nga.nyi ginggirrmagi?** [*What do you all think?*]

> *Sounds of agreement.* YILIMARRA *summons* JANDAMARRA *to come to him.*

YILIMARRA: [*to* JANDAMARRA, *smoothing his hair*] **Milawunagi winyunagi ngarragi.** [*Be my eyes and ears, boy.*]

JANDAMARRA: Yuwayi nyanyi. [*I will, uncle.*]

> YILIMARRA *exits, followed by the other* BUNUBA, *all saying their farewells to* JANDAMARRA *and* JINI.

MARRALAM: Dibinarra said, 'There's something about that boy'. But I didn't believe him. I know he'd just lost his father, but he was already a selfish little bugger before that, always getting Darrudi into trouble. But no-one listened to me. Dibinarra was boss for the law. Yilimarra was boss for everything else. I had to follow them. If it was up to me, we would have gone down and put spears in that Bligh mob the day they arrived.

> MARRALAM *turns on his heel and stalks off with the rest of the* BUNUBA MOB, *leaving* JINI *and* JANDAMARRA *very much alone.* JINI *very nervous,* JANDAMARRA *very excited, they approach* MARY *who has her back to them, busy with domestic chores.*

> MARY *turns and sees* JINI *and* JANDAMARRA, *standing stock still. She gasps in shock, but quickly composes herself and nods warily.*

JINI *remains rigid, her face expressionless, but* JANDAMARRA *breaks into a big, winning grin. After a small hesitation,* MARY *smiles back. She gestures him to come.*

MARY: What a smile you've got. Come on then. What do you want?

He walks past her and begins examining the camp things. She watches for a moment, then turns back to JINI.

[*Murmuring to herself*] Show no fear. [*To* JINI *and* JANDAMARRA] Hello. Do you speak English?

The women can only stare at each other. Behind MARY, JANDAMARRA *has found a rifle. He picks it up, wonderingly, just as* JOE *and* LINDSAY *enter.*

JOE: Hey there!

JOE *charges* JANDAMARRA *and snatches the rifle.* JINI *charges past* MARY *to protect her son. For a moment tragedy looms, until* MARY *steps between them.*

MARY: He meant no harm, Joe, I'm sure. He's just a boy.

JOE *lowers the rifle.*

Lindsay, grab that damper. See if they want some tucker.

LINDSAY *does this.* JANDAMARRA *eats.* LINDSAY *offers his hand.*

LINDSAY: I'm Lindsay, Lindsay Bl—

His words are cut off as JANDAMARRA *takes his arm, rubs his skin curiously.*

[*Laughing*] Come on then. I'll show you the horses.

The boys run off.

JINI: I agreed to be Yilimarra's spy… But from the moment Jandamarra grinned like that and ran off with Lindsay, I worried. He was always with Lindsay, not the other Bunuba kids who came into the station.

JINI *dons a maid's uniform as a projection and sound effects signal a time transition.*

Projected animation #2: Clouds passing quickly.

SCENE THREE

MARY: [*to the audience*] A bough shed, a sheep yard, a room with a roof. The work was backbreaking, and never ending. But our home grew around us.

JOE *runs on and whirls* MARY *around in a brief dance.*

JOE: Who'd've dared dream it, hey. The prettiest woman in the colony for me wife, a strapping young son, and a million acres to me name. A man should count his blessings.

MARY: [*giving him a kiss*] Not bad for a dairy lad from the backblocks of Bunbury, hey.

LINDSAY: And this is just the start, hey Dad.

JOE: Just the start, son. There's another million acres out there just waiting, once we get this place up an' running. And then another million, virgin country, out beyond that range.

Projected animation #3: Storm.

Lights down on all except JINI *as a crash of projection and wet season sound effects begins.*

JINI: It was all just jibber-jabber to me, but Jandamarra took in every word, learnt that new lingo. He fell in love with the new world.

The projection and sound effects continue, signalling a time transition.

SCENE FOUR

ALEXANDER FORREST *enters, passing a beer to* JOE *as he joins the* BLIGHS, *with* JINI *hovering in her maid's role, and* JANDAMARRA *drinking in the scene.*

FORREST: It's a celebration, boys!

LINDSAY: Our first wool clip shorn, on the wagons and ready to go.

JOE: [*ruffling* LINDSAY's *hair*] We're on our way, hey. There'll be no stopping us. Bigger'n the Duracks and the Lefroys, we'll be.

FORREST: One step at a time, my old friend. You say you had a mob perish when the spring dried up?

JOE: I'm still learning about this country.

FORREST: I know… but 'officially' the line on any stock losses is 'depredations by the natives'.

MARY: Jini, Pigeon, come with me.

MARY, JINI *and* JANDAMARRA *start to exit.*

FORREST: I'm pushing in the Parliament every chance I can to get more troopers up here, and I need all the ammunition I can get.

MARY: Lindsay. The horses.

LINDSAY: Sorry, Mr Forrest. Me and Pigeon've got to go check on the foals before dark.

JANDAMARRA *grins and runs in the other direction, towards the foals.* LINDSAY *chases after him, until stopped by* FORREST'*s voice.*

FORREST: Tell me, Lindsay. Do you fancy the idea of being one of the big men of the West with lots of stations like the Lefroys?

LINDSAY: I sure do. Me and Dad are going to buy you out of this place, and keep going from there.

JOE: [*trying to shut him up*] Lindsay!

FORREST: Unbridled ambition, I like it, Joe. [*To* LINDSAY] It's a grand enterprise we're engaged in, my boy. A grand enterprise. Five years ago I was the first white man to set foot in this country, and look at it now. Derby a town. A string of stations from the mouth of the Fitzroy for 150 miles inland. A thriving sheep trade.

LINDSAY: And more virgin country just waiting!

FORREST: That's the spirit.

JOE: And the Member for Kimberley has a finger in every pie, hey Alex.

FORREST: Why not, Joe? Why not?

JOE: Well, I'm telling you, this piece of your pie needs new troughs and tanks now.

FORREST: Let's wait and see what we get for this clip. And start looking, you two. Find more water. It's here in this country. It's gotta be.

JANDAMARRA *runs on, calling:*

JANDAMARRA: Ngarranyi! Balabalaawu. [*Mum! Hurry.*]

LINDSAY: Pigeon?

JANDAMARRA *ignores him, crossing the stage.*

JANDAMARRA: Wadbirali milawa Yilimarra. [*Come and see, it's Yilimarra.*]

A TROOPER *and an Aboriginal* TRACKER *appear. The* TRACKER
holds a chain, which is looped around the neck of YILIMARRA *and
two* OTHER MEN. *As* JANDAMARRA *exits* YILIMARRA *calls to him:*

YILIMARRA: Ngarranybulu.nga? [*Where's your mother?*]
TROOPER: [*whirling around*] Shut your gob, you mongrel.

The TROOPER *makes to clout* YILIMARRA, *but despite being hin-
dered by the chains,* YILIMARRA *confronts him. The two glare at
each other, and it is the* TROOPER *who blinks and steps back.*

FORREST: Looks like you've been doing a fine job there, Constable
McDonald.
TROOPER: [*saluting*] Mr Forrest sir. Thank you, sir. Joe, where'll I put
this lot?
JOE: That bloodwood near the stables, Mac. Keep them away from the
blacks' camp.
TROOPER: No worries. [*To the* TRACKER] Chain him tight, Sambo.
TRACKER: Yes, boss.

They start to cross the stage. FORREST *moves to inspect the prisoners more closely. He stops as* YILIMARRA, *glowers at him.*

FORREST: Is this cheeky bastard the Ellemarra they all talk about? The
king of the sheep thieves.
TROOPER: Sure is. The devil himself.

JINI *and* JANDAMARRA *run on, followed shortly by* MARY, *who
hovers anxiously by* LINDSAY.

JINI: Nginyjaga-nhi? [*What happened?*]

YILIMARRA *jerks against the chain as he turns to* JINI.

YILIMARRA: [*bitterly*] Banggawuwindantha nganggi ngawiy-nhungu-
way guda. [*They shot your auntie and her husband.*]

JINI *begins to wail. The* TRACKER *leads the prisoners off.* FORREST,
JOE *and the* TROOPER *follow, with backslapping and smiles.*

MARY: [*distressed*] What did he just say to you, Jini?

JINI *turns to* MARY, *but does not answer. Her wailing does not
stop, and she runs off in the direction of the prisoners.*

JANDAMARRA: They killed her auntie and uncle.

Brushing off LINDSAY*'s uncertain approach,* JANDAMARRA *follows* JINI, *leaving* MARY *in shock.* LINDSAY *takes a step towards his mother. Neither knows what to say. He turns and follows the others off.*

Projected animation #4: Short storm.

JINI*'s wailing fades into a transition of wet season effects: projection, thunder rolling and flashes of lightning.*

MARY *shakes herself and turns to the audience. As she speaks* JANDAMARRA *enters, stalking, then poises in a crouch.* LINDSAY *follows a few paces behind, carrying a rifle. He takes a careful step. The sound of a snapping twig.* JANDAMARRA *looks around, annoyed, a finger to his lips.*

MARY: They were inseparable... Lindsay was older than Pigeon. But when they were on their own, Pigeon was the leader. I never said anything to Joe of course, but I could see it. He could run faster, ride better, shoot straighter. Most of the time, it was Lindsay following Pigeon.

The transition effects continue into:

SCENE FIVE

Projected animation #5: Thinner snake sleeping.

JANDAMARRA *takes a cautious step forward. And another. Without turning, he signals* LINDSAY *to come forward.* LINDSAY *comes up level with* JANDAMARRA, *raising the rifle in the direction* JANDAMARRA *points...* Bang!

LINDSAY: [*pointing*] He's gone in that little valley past the boab there.

JANDAMARRA *frowns unhappily.*

You can follow his tracks, hey? We can still get him.
JANDAMARRA: He'll be gone now.
LINDSAY: How do you know?

JANDAMARRA *just shrugs.*

We should have a look up there—might be a spring or something.
JANDAMARRA: [*nervously*] I don't know that place.

LINDSAY: I thought you knew all this country.

JANDAMARRA: [*steering* LINDSAY *away*] Come on. Mister Bligh said we've gotta check that fence further up.

LINDSAY: [*looking back in the direction he shot*] We've got all day. Come on, let's go look.

JANDAMARRA: [*panicky*] No! Can't go there. Danger place; got a big snake, Yilimbirri Unggud. Come on. I'll show you another place.

> JANDAMARRA *takes off.*

LINDSAY: Pigeon! Wait up…

> *But* JANDAMARRA *keeps going, and* LINDSAY *follows. They disappear…*

> *The lights change.*

> *Projected animation #6: Bululu with white cockatoos.*

> *Bush noises, then the sound of a stream, and Bululu animation representing a lush waterhole and birds. The boys re-emerge,* JANDAMARRA *leading.* LINDSAY *is wide-eyed as he looks around.*

JANDAMARRA: This is it. Bululu.

> *He bends and picks up a pebble, tosses it. Splash. He rubs a hand under each armpit, then gets down on his knees and swishes his hands.*

Bululu ngayini ngindaji Jandamarra. Ngindaji malngarri buga wadjay jarra nhingi, yingiy nhi Lindsay. **Ngindaji-yuwa yathaway.** [*Bululu, it's me, Jandamarra. This white boy with me, his name is Lindsay. He comes from a different place. Long way. But **he's stopping here now.***]

> *He looks up at* LINDSAY *expectantly.* LINDSAY *looks puzzled.* JANDAMARRA *puts a hand to each armpit.* LINDSAY *kneels down beside him and mimics his actions.*

This place got a snake too. Bululu we call him. He's a friendly one though. Not like Yilimbirri Unggud back there.

LINDSAY: What're you talking about?

JANDAMARRA: Yilimbirri Unggud, he made all this country. He's like the big boss for everything—really strong and dangerous.

LINDSAY *straightens, looking around rather nervously.*
JANDAMARRA *sits back, amused, watching him.*

[*Teasing*] How'd you miss that roo back there? You were close enough
to use a spear.

LINDSAY: Like you can use a spear.

JANDAMARRA: Of course I can. I have to when they make me a man.

LINDSAY *sits back beside him, looking puzzled.*

LINDSAY: 'Make you a man'?

JANDAMARRA *thinks for a moment, and decides 'why not'.*

JANDAMARRA: Everyone's gotta dance and sing for me, and they'll put
me through the law.

LINDSAY: What?

JANDAMARRA: I'll get that law for Yilimbirri. But first I gotta learn big
mob of songs and other stuff. And I gotta track and spear an old man
kangaroo on my own. [*He thinks.*] What about you? How do they
make you a man?

LINDSAY: [*stumped, he thinks*] Buggered if I know… So when's this
going to happen?

JANDAMARRA: Should've been this wet season just finished. But them
old men said to wait till Yilimarra comes back from jail in Roebourne.

LINDSAY: Ellemara! That one Forrest called the king of the sheep thieves!
Dad says he's the worst bastard of the lot.

JANDAMARRA: [*turning to look* LINDSAY *in the eye*] He's my uncle.
He's got to be there when they put me through that law.

LINDSAY: What's he like?

JANDAMARRA: He's the strongest, bravest man. He can beat anyone.

LINDSAY: Not my old man he couldn't.

A beat, as the boys exchange looks. LINDSAY *changes the subject.*

Does this creek run all year?

JANDAMARRA: Yeah, there's a spring in that hill up there. It never runs
dry. [*Pointing*] Two little fences there and there, and you'll be right.
Won't need any pipe or trough or anything.

LINDSAY: Wait till Dad sees this!

He runs out, followed by JANDAMARRA. *This segues into the next
scene.*

SCENE SIX

LINDSAY *and* JOE *enter Lillimooloora as* JOE *packs.*

LINDSAY: [*excited*] All it needs is two little block fences. We won't need pipes or troughs or anything.

JOE: I'll ride out with you and look it over, soon as I get back from this trip to Derby. It sounds like just what we need. Well done, son.

LINDSAY: Pigeon was telling me how Rainbow snakes live in the waterholes and places like that. And they're *really* big—like a house or something. He reckons some of them are really dangerous, but not the one at this spring. He reckons they created all this land—like God did in Genesis. [*He laughs.*] 'That seven day story', he called it.

Enjoying the story, LINDSAY *does not notice the change in* JOE*'s mood.*

JOE: Don't you go comparing that native mumbo jumbo to the Good Book! You're spending too much time with that boy.

LINDSAY: He showed me that spring, Dad. There might be others.

JOE: Bah.

MARY *enters, waving a cheque book, smiling.*

MARY: Sign it! I've written the cheque out!

LINDSAY: Yes!

JOE: [*excited, yet hesitant*] Are you sure? If we don't make the budget on the next clip we could be struggling…

MARY: I've done the sums. I've allowed for the school fees. And the boat fare, and an allowance. It's tight, but we can do it. I just told you, sign the cheque!

The three BLIGHS *embrace in high excitement.* JOE *breaks away.*

JOE: It's a big step.

MARY: We've got to take the plunge soon, or we'll never be free of Forrest.

JOE: I don't trust him.

MARY: The contract is clear as day. You've got the right to make the offer, and he's got no grounds to refuse it.

JOE: But one bad season… we could lose everything.

LINDSAY: What if we put off my schooling for another year, that'll save some money? [*Getting carried away as he talks up the idea*] Who wants to go to Perth anyway! You need me here, Dad, and Mum's teaching me good.

MARY & JOE: [*together*] No!

JOE: Teaching me good! Listen to yourself. You're going to get the learning I never had, like it or not.

A babble of argument erupts, until MARY *overrides the other two.*

MARY: Settle down, everybody. We don't want you to go, love, but it's beyond time for you to be getting a proper education. Joe, sign this and get on your way, or you won't get to Lennard River before dark.

JOE: [*signing*] You're right, as always. Here we are on the verge of our great dream, and I'm snappy as a lady's lap dog.

JINI *and* JANDAMARRA *enter, crossing the stage.*

JANDAMARRA: Have a good trip, Mr Bligh. [*To* LINDSAY] Maaningarri milawinya. [*See you tomorrow.*]

LINDSAY: Yaninyja jimarri. [*See you.*]

JOE *turns on* LINDSAY.

JOE: What did you say?!

LINDSAY: [*nervously*] Yaninyja jimarri. It means 'see you, mate'.

JOE: [*heavily emphasised*] Don't you ever let me hear you talking that blackfeller lingo again! Ever!

LINDSAY *hangs his head.*

MARY: Hey there, snappy.

JOE: He needs to understand that he's a white man. With responsibilities. You look after your mum while I'm away. You're the manager while I'm not here, so try acting like it, instead of hanging around with that native boy all day long.

LINDSAY: I'll make you proud of me, Dad. You'll see.

JOE *exits first.* LINDSAY *rejects* MARY*'s attempt to comfort him as he also leaves.*

SCENE SEVEN

Morning. LINDSAY *enters, carrying horse gear, rifle and shovel.* JANDAMARRA *runs on, chasing him.*

JANDAMARRA: Where we going today, Lindsay?

LINDSAY: [*curtly*] I'm going for a ride.

JANDAMARRA: [*taken aback by his tone*] Which way?

LINDSAY: Dunno yet.

JANDAMARRA: What's the gun for?

LINDSAY: None of your bloody business. Enough of the bloody questions, alright.

JANDAMARRA: Is something wrong? Did I do something?

LINDSAY *shoulders his gear and keeps walking.*

LINDSAY: [*harshly, without turning*] Yaninyja.

JANDAMARRA: Where you going?

LINDSAY *exits.*

Lindsay?!

JANDAMARRA *begins pacing, clearly worried.*

DIBINARRA *and* MARRALAM *enter with* YILIMARRA, *who has a manacle and chain dangling from one arm.*

DIBINARRA: Nginyji Roebourne nhingi ma biragganggayali? [*You've come back from Roebourne?*]

YILIMARRA: Yuwana gilinymana barrba wan.ngay. [*I've been walking for a month.*]

MARRALAM: **Nginyji girrgayraymi. Ngalabani jalangurru ma?** [***You're the first one to escape. Are the others alright?***]

YILIMARRA: Ngayi jalanggurru. Burmangarri jalanggurru ma Jini-way Jandamarra? [*Not good. Tell me, how are Jini and Jandamarra?*]

MARRALAM: **Dawunggawunmagi malngarri nyirraji.ingga buga.** [***The boy likes living with the white men.***]

DIBINARRA: **Nginyji ban.ganggayali.nhir, wina gurama wuni.** [*Can we take him for the law now?*]

YILIMARRA: Yuwai… Wadbirali, ngindaji yilagama ngarragi. [*Come on, get this thing off me.*]

MARRALAM *brings a tomahawk down hard on a link of chain.*

MARY *enters and sees* JANDAMARRA, *still agitated.*

MARY: What is it, Pigeon?

JANDAMARRA: [*nervously*] Missus Bligh, did Lindsay tell you where he was going?

MARY: He said something about looking for a new spring.

JANDAMARRA *backs away, trying to compose himself.*

[*Seeing his alarm*] Is something wrong?… Pigeon?

JANDAMARRA: No. Nothing, Missus Bligh, nothing.

JANDAMARRA *runs off.* MARY *watches him, puzzled.*

Projected animation #7: Big snake sleeping.

LINDSAY *enters cautiously, carrying a rifle and a shovel. He shades his eyes with a hand and peers intently.*

LINDSAY: That's got to be another spring… All that green there… Bugger you, Pigeon, keeping this to yourself. I'm not scared of some bloody snake.

He moves on, swallowing nervously. He sees the beauty within.

Yes, water! Just like I thought.

He excitedly scoops a handful of water, tastes it, grins. He turns and looks appraisingly.

Few lengths of pipe. Trough down there. Beautiful. Just need to shift this to let it flow properly.

He tries to shift a rock, but it won't budge.

There is a flicker of a projected snake image and a low, strange sound.

JINI *enters from the homestead with a basket of washing, just as there is a great gust of wind. She drops the basket and looks at the sky.*

JINI: Ngunda gaman.ginyjawu? [*Who are you looking for?*]

The lights change as the axe work becomes loud again. MARRALAM *works on* YILIMARRA*'s chains. Suddenly* DIBINARRA *grimaces and hunches over, rubbing at his chest.*

YILIMARRA: Nginyjaga nhi? [*Are you alright?*]

> DIBINARRA *looks around, puzzled, but shrugs it off.*
>
> JANDAMARRA *enters from the same direction as* LINDSAY *did, hands over his ears, looking panicked. He takes a couple of steps towards the gateway.*

LINDSAY: This is perfect. Bugger you, Pigeon, keeping this to yourself. I don't care if you are there, snake.

> *He rubs a rock under his arm and then up his bum and tosses it into the water.*

This is the Blighs' waterhole! Joe Bligh and son! Piss off, snake. This is Lindsay's waterhole. Bligh's Bombey Hole. Piss off!

> *He jumps into the water. A loud splash. The snake sound screams loud and urgent.*
>
> *Projected animation #8: Snake bright and fat… moves away from right to left… a crossfade from #7.*
>
> JANDAMARRA *looks around wildly. He drops to his knees.*

JANDAMARRA: [*calling desperately*] Lindsay!

> *The snake sound reaches a climax.*
>
> JANDAMARRA *cowers on the ground in sheer, icy terror. The women shrink back.* DIBINARRA *grabs his chest and falls. There are screams and shouts and wind and the slithering of the snake.*
>
> *The lights focus on* JANDAMARRA *as he struggles to his feet and begins to stagger towards where* LINDSAY *disappeared. Out of the noise come words, deep and growling.*

YILIMBIRRI UNGGUD: **Bilirri nganggi urugawuwila… Guju nganggi udgalha!** [*I will take your spirit! Your bones will be lost!*]

> JANDAMARRA *collapses. There is a roaring of wind, and a screeching of birds, as the snake image dominates, before disappearing upwards.*
>
> *Everyone has run from the stage except* JANDAMARRA, *still cowering on the ground, shivering with fear, and* MARY *who is silently weeping.*

Silence. Then WANGAMARRA:

WANGAMARRA: [*sung*] Winyjiwi ma mara marangayidi, Winyjiwi ma
   mara marangayidi
   Dilibiya ma mara marangayidi, Dilibiya ma mara marangayidi.

This song continues, at a lower volume as LINDSAY's *body is carried on stage, and under the next scenes.*

SCENE EIGHT

Lights up on MARY, *front of stage.*

MARY: An emptiness opened up inside me. And it's never been filled.

*She retreats to where a body lies beneath a blanket on a table. She
kneels, grief-stricken, stroking, hugging the body.*

Lights up on JINI *as she crouches over* JANDAMARRA *and strokes
him soothingly. She looks up when* YILIMARRA *and* DIBINARRA
enter, and moves front of stage to join them.

YILIMARRA: [*hissing, face close to* JINI's] **Nhi.ingga ma wadgira
   malngarri buga nyirrajiyuwa?** [*Did he take the white boy there?*]

JINI: Ngayi! **Nhi.ingga mi nhi yathawura.** [*No! He tried to stop him.*]

DIBINARRA: **Yillimbirri Unggud milu lirrbawu.** [*Yillimbirri Unggud
   is angry.*] Thangani yunggawudagi. **Maningga lamajgawudagi.**
   [*His uncles have sent word. Tonight he will be taken to prepare
   for the law.*]

   JINI *lets out a wail, as* YILIMARRA *and* DIBINARRA *exit. The song
   continues, briefly a little louder.* MARRALAM *and another man pull*
   JANDAMARRA *to his feet and lead him off.*

JINI: There was something wrong with my boy, but he wouldn't tell me
   what. They took him away to prepare him for his man-making. I left
   too. It was a long time before I went back to the station.

   The song continues, but at a lower volume.

   JINI *exits, as* JOE *storms on, then comes to a sudden halt at the
   body of his son. He lifts a corner of the blanket. Looks. Recoils.
   He turns to* MARY. *They embrace fiercely, clinging to each other.
   Eventually they separate.*

JOE: He fell? An accident?

MARY *nods.*

I don't believe it. Pigeon was with him, hey? Where is he now?

MARY: Down at the camp, I suppose.

JOE: I'll get the truth out of him.

He makes to leave but MARY *steps in front of him.*

MARY: We bury our son tomorrow, Joseph. It will be done with dignity. No inquisitions until after the funeral.

They turn back to the body. The singing becomes loud again as MARY *and* JOE *place a white cross for Lindsay's grave.*

WANGAMARRA: [*sung*] Winyjiwi ma mara marangayidi, Winyjiwi ma mara marangayidi
Dilibiya ma mara marangayidi, Dilibiya ma mara marangayidi.

SCENE NINE

Bush. DIBINARRA, YILIMARRA *and* MARRALAM *enter with* DARRUDI. JANDAMARRA *trails on slowly behind them.* DIBINARRA *gestures to* YILIMARRA, *who goes back to* JANDAMARRA.

YILIMARRA: Ba. Wadbirali. [*Come on.*]

JANDAMARRA *does not hurry.*

DIBINARRA: **Nginyjaga nhi ngayi wilayinbi. Malngarri ma burrudi ling.nginyja?** [*What's wrong, you won't speak to us? Are you still thinking about the white boy?*]

JANDAMARRA *just looks at the ground. Until, exasperated,* YILIMARRA *seizes his chin and forces him to look.*

YILIMARRA: [*insistent*] Buma ngarragi. Nginyjaga-nhi? [*Tell me. What is wrong?*]

JANDAMARRA *wrenches free and glares at them all.*

JANDAMARRA: **Bilirri nganggi urugawuwila! Guju nganggi udgalha!** [*I will take your spirit! Your bones will be lost!*]

DIBINARRA *gasps. He reaches out to* JANDAMARRA, *who backs away.*

DIBINARRA: Yilimbirri Unggud! [*The Yilimbirri snake!*]

JANDAMARRA: Yuwayi! Mi ngarragi yiningga! [*Yes! That's what he told me!*]

JANDAMARRA *takes a step backwards, but* DIBINARRA *intercepts him and draws him in close, almost cradling him.*

DIBINARRA: Ngarragi buga. **Yarri.ingga gurrijbinya.** [*My boy, my boy.* **We will take care of you.**]

JANDAMARRA *breaks free of* DIBINARRA *and glares at him and* YILIMARRA.

JANDAMARRA: Nginyjaga?! **Bilanyi nyirraji, ngayi wiyganyjiya ngarraginhi.** Garrgawinbu. [*What?!* **You can't protect me from him! Leave me alone.**]

JANDAMARRA *runs off, leaving the men bewildered.*

MARRALAM *turns to the audience as* DIBINARRA *and* YILIMARRA *follow* JANDAMARRA.

MARRALAM: At first I thought it was some sick joke Jandamarra was playing. But Dibinarra convinced me. And the fear in the kid's eyes. That was real. None of us knew what to think. There were stories of the Unggud snakes talking to men. Old stories. But to a boy? Never. Yilimarra kept telling Jandamarra he was special, that he must have some sort of power for him to hear the Unggud speaking to him. But he wasn't listening.

BUNUBA MEN *usher* DARRUDI *and a listless* JANDAMARRA *on, and gently seat them. Singing begins.*

All the clans were gathering for the ceremony for him and Darrudi. But there was an uneasy feeling in the camp. We got word that a big police patrol was sniffing around to the south, but we had to go ahead. Jandamarra did everything he was supposed to do. But he was… spiritless. We were in the men's camp, waiting for the big dance that night to finish the man-making.

ILAJI *runs on, yelling.*

ILAJI: Limbaawu! Wathila wadgurragali! [*Police! Coming up close!*]

Pandemonium. The sounds of rifle fire and the cries of women, as the men grab their spears. A TROOPER *runs on shouting and firing.*

A BUNUBA MAN *goes down. The* TROOPER *shouts at* YILIMARRA *and* ILAJI *to drop their weapons. Eventually they do, and the* TROOPER *turns his attention to* JANDAMARRA, *who has not moved.*

TROOPER: Get up!…

Still JANDAMARRA *sits.*

GET… UP!

The TROOPER *forces* JANDAMARRA *to his feet, then herds the* MEN *off at gunpoint, as* JINI *enters.*

JINI: I'd escaped from the station, but everything had turned to rubbish. The land was sick and Jandamarra lost to us… that day at Yilimbirri spring when Lindsay died. And then lost again, taken away to Derby with Yilimarra and the others. I thought I might never see my son again.

MARY *steps forward.*

MARY: I took off down south, just to get away. When I got on that boat, I thought I might never come back. But I discovered Perth had become a foreign country to me. I longed for those cliffs… And to be close to Lindsay.

Sounds effect a time transition.

SCENE TEN

Lillimooloora. RICHARDSON *walks on wearily. He stops by the white cross, shifts his swag from one shoulder to another, spits.* JOE *is watching.*

RICHARDSON: Another one bites the dust.

JOE: What brings you this way, stranger? [*Calling off*] Mayannie! Visitor! Bring us some tea!

RICHARDSON *ambles up to join him, and slings his swag down.*

RICHARDSON: I'm on me way to Derby from Halls Creek. Thought I'd check out the back country on me way through.

JOE: Prospecting, were you?

RICHARDSON: Tried me hand.

JOE: Gold is for fools and Chinamen. Stock is where the future lies up here. Sheep and cattle.

RICHARDSON: This is your place?

JOE: Yep.

RICHARDSON: It's nice country… Joe, isn't it? Joe Bligh?

He offers his hand and they shake.

Bill Richardson.

JOE: See any bush blacks roundabout?

RICHARDSON: Not a one.

JOE: [*with a laugh*] It's been quiet since the coppers cleaned up a big mob a few months back. Caught 'em while they were having one of their big singsongs. Put their ringleader and a mob of others away for spearing stock. One of 'em was a little git that we fed and clothed right here. Treacherous little sod. But I'm still on me guard. A man should know his enemy I reckon. You wouldn't believe what they get up to. There's one of them witchdoctors out there, he grinds up bones—human bones—and slips it into his victim's tucker. They're evil bastards I tell you. You heard any stories from up Hall's Creek way?

RICHARDSON: I keep meself to meself.

JOE: Don't mind yer own company then?

RICHARDSON: You could say that.

JOE: Done any stock work?

RICHARDSON: Bit here and there.

JOE: Any plans?

RICHARDSON *shakes his head.* MAYANNIE, *a beauty in her late teens wearing a maid's uniform, enters with pannikins of tea.* RICHARDSON's *eyes take in* MAYANNIE. *Out of* JOE's *line of sight, she smiles at him.*

MAYANNIE: Wajin ub binis na boj. Ei gan goabag cam nou? [*The washing-up's finished, boss. Can I go back to camp now?*]

JOE: Go on.

MAYANNIE *exits, with* RICHARDSON *watching.*

I'm starting up another run further down the range, Brooking Springs. Moving into cattle, so's I can play both markets. I'm looking for a man to take care of this place for us.

RICHARDSON: [*interested*] Yeah?

SCENE ELEVEN

MARY *enters.*

MARY: While I was away Joe did the deal to get a new lease, at Brooking Springs. He tried to tell me it would do me good, getting away from Lillimooloora, with all its memories. It was him that couldn't stand it though. He'd changed when I got back. It was like the bones of his soul had broken, and then set again all twisted and crooked.

SCENE TWELVE

Derby jail. ILAJI *and* YILIMARRA *sit cross-legged on the floor.* JANDAMARRA *sits, knees drawn up, turned away from them. The three are linked by neck chains.* ILAJI *chews at a bone.* YILIMARRA *swallows, then nudges* JANDAMARRA *and pushes a tin plate towards him.*

YILIMARRA: Ngabawu. [*Eat.*]

JANDAMARRA: Ngayi ngirrginyi dayinbi. [*Not hungry.*]

YILIMARRA: **Girrgarawanmagi.** Ngayini jangi girrgaralimi Rawubun nhingi. [***We'll all escape from here.** Like when I ran away from Roebourne.*]

JANDAMARRA: [*shaking his chains at* YILIMARRA] **Yajilinggira!** [***You're dreaming.***]

Ngindaji-yuwa ngayini yathawungay? [***Anyway, who said I want to go back to the bush?***]

ILAJI: Ngayi wilanyjima yiningga, nyirraji nyaanyi nganggi. Nginyji ngayi gurama. [*Don't talk to your uncle that way. You're not even a proper man yet.*]

YILIMARRA: Ngayi wilanyjima Ilaji. Ngayi barurru bujani. [*Shut up, Ilaji. It's not his fault that the ceremony was cut short.*]

JANDAMARRA: [*to* YILIMARRA] Ngayi! Nginyjanyi! **Thayjin-nhingi wurugayinma, nyirraji nhi limba-ingga wadbayinmagi!** [*No! You're the one! **You drag me away from the station, and we get caught by the police!***]

He tears frustratedly at the chains, as if to remove them.

Nga thirrili ngarragi, nginyjinyja jimiy ngarragi? [***Where's that**

power of mine you talked about?] Mariy wa̱dbanyjima. **Ngindaji yatha̱ngira ja̱nga ja̱nga ̱ngarri.** [*You're lying. I'm sitting here in chains.*]

> *As* JA̱NDAMARRA *speaks, a white* TROOPER *and a black* TRACKER *in police uniforms enter. The* TRACKER *gestures at* JA̱NDAMARRA *who has turned his back.*

TRACKER: [*to the* TROOPER] He can ride, that one. Used to work for Joe Bligh. Good English too he gottim. Better'n me.

TROOPER: He's an angry bugger. What name?

TRACKER: Pigeon.

TROOPER: Boy!

> *No response.*

Pigeon.

> *He half turns, looking sullen, ignoring* ILAJI'*s scowl, and* YILIMARRA'*s warning look.*

Fancy working in the stables? A tryout. Looking after the police horses.

> *Now he faces them.*

JA̱NDAMARRA: I get out of here if I say yes?

TROOPER: If y'do the job proper, and stop out of trouble.

JA̱NDAMARRA: Yuwayi.

> *The* TRACKER *releases* JA̱NDAMARRA *from his chains. He steps away from the prisoners, putting on a tracker's jacket.*

ILAJI: Tharra! [*Dog!*]

YILIMARRA: Garrgawu. Wa̱dbay Ilaji. [*Leave him alone. Let him go, Ilaji.*]

> *Lights down on the* PRISONERS *as the* TRACKER *shuts them up, and hustles them off.* JINI *enters.*

JINI: When their time was done, Yilimarra and the others made the long walk home. But Ja̱ndamarra stayed in Derby, working for the police. He was running away from Yilimbirri U̱nggud, the snake that spoke to him. Poor feller my son. Five years it took him to get up the nerve to come ba̲ck.

She exits, shaking her head sadly as projection and effects signal a time transition.

Projected animation #9: Full storm

SCENE THIRTEEN

Derby police yard, night. As the thunder and lightning effects continue MINGO MICK *sits, self-contained.* JANDAMARRA *enters, somewhat nervously.*

JANDAMARRA: [*timid*] Are you that Mingo Mick?

> MINGO MICK*'s nod is almost imperceptible.*

Yoo thu wun bin gedim thud lud mirdru init? [*You caught that lot of murderers, hey?*]

MINGO MICK: Ie donoa hoo mirdru. Ie jis gidim orlubud. [*I don't know if they're murderers. I just catch them.*]

JANDAMARRA: Yoo bin bolurim man riet thooroo dejid indid? [*You tracked them right through the desert, hey?*]

> *Silence…*

> JANDAMARRA *tries again.*

Orlud regin yoo numba wun draga orl roun la dijun gundree. [*Everybody says you're the best tracker in the whole country.*]

> *More silence.*

I wanna be a tracker.

MINGO MICK: You don't want to be a tracker.

JANDAMARRA: You get a coat, a horse, a rifle…

> MINGO MICK *chuckles to himself.*

You get respect from the gudia.

> MINGO MICK *gives him a knowing smile.*

MINGO MICK: Wijai bamlee belonga yoo libin? [*Where's your family living?*]

JANDAMARRA: My mum's living out bush.

MINGO MICK: I'm tellin' you, you don't want to be a tracker, young feller.
You gotta go home.

JANDAMARRA: I don't want to live longa bush.

MINGO MICK *turns, gives* JANDAMARRA *his full attention, looking him up and down.*

MINGO MICK: You're scared. What you scared of?

JANDAMARRA: [*unnerved*] Bullshit. I'm not scared of nothing.

SCENE FOURTEEN

Lilimooloora. JANDAMARRA *walks over to the white cross, not noticing* RICHARDSON *and* MAYANNIE *enter. After a few moments' contemplation he squats and scoops up a handful of earth.* RICHARDSON *draws a revolver from his belt. He grins at* MAYANNIE'*s alarm. He aims over* JANDAMARRA'*s head, and fires!*

JANDAMARRA *stifles his shock, and turns calmly.*

JANDAMARRA: What the hell was that for?

RICHARDSON: [*impressed*] Cool customer, hey?

They eye each other for a moment. RICHARDSON *smiles.* JANDAMARRA *holds his look a moment longer, then smiles back.*

Joe told me to shoot any blackfeller that comes near the grave.

JANDAMARRA: Nobody told me.

RICHARDSON: Well, now you know. [*He chuckles.*] Anyway, you're supposed to be down at the horse yards getting ready. We'll see if you're as good at horsebreaking as you say.

He gives MAYANNIE *an affectionate pat on the bum as he heads inside.*

JANDAMARRA: Ee brobu funeewun thud bugu. Wud kien im? [*Funny bugger, isn't he? What's he like?*]

MAYANNIE: Ee ried. Ee maigem mee larb… jumdiem. [*He's alright. He makes me laugh… sometimes.*]

JANDAMARRA: Ay wiyi. Ngarragima bulba wurrgaya mayaruyuwa? [*Hey, girl. Did you put that mattress in the quarters for me?*]

MAYANNIE: Juralinhi bagaray. Mindili ngarri. [*It's been there for ages. It's got fleas.*]

JANDAMARRA: **Walay-yuwa mayaru yatha-ngira. Malngarri-jangi.** [*I've got my own little house, just like a white man.*] [*With a wink*]

Mudbee ie gidim woomin blu_ngu wujbulu negswan. [*Maybe I'll get the whitefeller's woman next.*]

MAYANNIE: Don gid jigi, ee mied jendim yoo bag lu gam... Or mudbee ie dulim. [*Don't get cheeky, or he might send you down to the camp... Or I might tell him to.*]

A beat, as they look at each other.

Hou long yoo gurru jiddoun iyar? [*How long are you staying?*]

JANDAMARRA: Ul jis dooim dijun horsbraigin job birs, den jinggubud. [*I'll do this horsebreaking job first, then think about it.*]

SCENE FIFTEEN

Night. JANDAMARRA *returns to the cross. He squats, scoops up a handful of earth and scatters it over the grave. He turns to see* JINI *coming down from the ranges, pulling an ugly station dress on. They run to each other and embrace fiercely.*

JINI: Warraa! Ngalaganyi _ngarragi. [*My boy.*]

JANDAMARRA: Ngarrinyi. [*Mum.*]

They disengage, smiling hugely at each other.

JINI: Juraali warigaywanu. **Gilandirri ban.ganggayali.** Jalungurruma yathanggira? [*You've been gone a long time, son.* **You've come back big, like a man.** *Are you well?*]

JANDAMARRA: Mmm, jalangurru. [*Mmm, well enough.*]

JINI *fidgets, pulling at the dress she is wearing.*

JINI: Aagha. Ngindaji dreedi ganday nyinggarana. [*Aah. This dress is no good. It's making me itchy.*]

JANDAMARRA: [*plucking at his shirt and trousers*] We gotta wear clothes if we're livin' with the whitefellers.

JINI: **Nginyjagawu yathawu ngay ngindaji-yuwa! Longa wujpela.** [**Why would I want to stay here! With the whitefellers.**]

JANDAMARRA: This place is okay.

JINI: Wina linginyja ngindaji muwayi walaynhi? Mayaru ngay-ngarri, malngarri ngay-ngarri? [*Can you remember this place when you were little? When there were no houses, no white people.*]

He looks away from her.

Dibinarra-ingga ling.nga ngarri muwayi. [*Dibinarra is worrying for the country.*]

JANDAMARRA: It's still here.

JINI: [*annoyed at his flippancy*] Muwayi yarrangi, **malayiguda, malngarri-ingga dun.gawurrmagi.** [*Our country, even our Dreaming places are getting covered up by the whitefellers.*]

JANDAMARRA: That's not my fault.

JINI: **Ngayima ban.ganggurangi-yali? Muwayi yawu?** [*Why won't you come back to us? To our country?*]

JANDAMARRA: [*fiercely*] **Ngayini milhalba. Ngayi girrgarawulimi wanyjirri-jangi—malngarrinhi.** [*I'm a hunter. I won't run away from the white man like a kangaroo.*]

> They glare at each other. JINI *seems to be about to say something, but holds back.*
>
> JANDAMARRA *backs away from her, his glare changing to a look of torment. She reaches a hand out to him. But he shakes his head, turns towards the station, and exits.*
>
> JINI *stands there, hand extended.*
>
> *Time transition.*

SCENE SIXTEEN

Projected animation #10: Bululu.

JANDAMARRA *and* RICHARDSON *enter.*

RICHARDSON: Wire Spring, hey.

JANDAMARRA: Bululu, we call it.

RICHARDSON: [*looking around, appreciating the beauty*] It's… it's not bad. Why haven't you shown me this place before?

JANDAMARRA: Can't give away all me secrets straight up. But this is the only pool that's still got enough water for a swim this time of year.

RICHARDSON: [*peeling off his shirt*] Know what you mean. Damn fixing fences in this weather. Dunno why we flog ourselves like this, making old Joe rich.

JANDAMARRA: You can bugger off any time, can't you?

RICHARDSON: To what? This life suits me—king of me own little empire.

JANDAMARRA: Isn't Joe Bligh the king?

RICHARDSON: You are a cheeky blackfeller, aren't you? S'pose he is. I'll have to settle for Duke, hey? Duke Richardson, Lord of Lillimooloora! Or should I be Earl? What you reckon?

JANDAMARRA: Which one's bigger boss? Duke or Earl?

RICHARDSON: Buggered if I know.

JANDAMARRA: Take your pick then.

RICHARDSON: [*with a laugh*] Earl I reckon. It's got a better ring to it. [*He laughs again.*] That'll go down well with the boys in Derby... Earl Richardson. [*He looks to the skies.*] I don't like the look of those clouds building up, mate. Reckon me an' May might bail for town in a couple of days, make sure we get through before the storms. I don't fancy putting in the whole frigging wet season here.

JANDAMARRA: [*startled*] What? Mayannie's going too?

RICHARDSON: Course. Need someone to wash me shirts an' sober me up once a week. I'll set her up at the combo camp there behind the Chinaman's store.

JANDAMARRA: [*worried*] You are coming back after the wet, hey?

RICHARDSON: If they haven't locked me up by then. Hey, don't worry. I'll be back. Just make sure you're still here.

JANDAMARRA: Where am I gonna go?

SCENE SEVENTEEN

Brooking Springs, night. JOE *approaches* MARY *hesitantly.*

JOE: D'you ever still get the hankering for a piano, Mary?

MARY: [*surprised by the question*] Not for a long time now.

JOE: You used to play so beautifully.

MARY: Mmm.

> JOE *moves closer and begins to knead her shoulders. She relaxes. He bends to nuzzle her neck. She masks her surprise, as she leans back into him, enjoying the moment.*

What's brought this on?

JOE: [*taking her hand*] I've been thinking, Mary.

MARY: [*playfully*] Yes?

JOE: Things are going well. One more good season and we're going to be set. Listen, I know we've had our... [*searching for a word*] setbacks—

MARY: Setback!? Is that what you call it? Our son dying?

JOE: No word is big enough, Mary… What I'm trying to say to you is that we're within reach of what we always dreamed of: a string of stations big enough to get through the toughest times, to last for generations! A piano if you want one… and…

MARY: And what, Joe?

JOE: It's not too late, is it? You know… for you… Couldn't we think about… [*Finally managing to blurt it out*] about trying for another son?

MARY: [*storming to her feet*] It's not me you want, is it?! You just need a breeder, like those bloody heifers out there you drool over. I'd be lucky to survive the carrying of a child at my age. That wouldn't bother you though, would it, as long as I pushed out an heir for your damned empire?!

JOE: Aah. I should have held my tongue.

MARY: You should have.

JOE: You're addled, woman. You're soft in the head, and soft in the heart for all but me. You even took Richardson's side about keeping Pigeon on.

MARY: All I ever said was that he was a friend to Lindsay.

JOE: He was there when our son died, and the next morning he'd vanished. Can't you do the sums?! [*Bitterly*] And now he's back there at Lillimooloora.

Lights down. Lightning flickers. Distant thunder.

SCENE EIGHTEEN

When the lights fade up, as JINI *speaks,* JANDAMARRA *stares towards the ranges. He takes off his boots, gets up, hesitantly stomps a few steps of dance. He looks out at the ranges again. He takes off his shirt, picks up a spear, testing its weight.*

JINI: He walked into our camp like he'd never been away. Proud as anything as he threw a big old man kangaroo down at my feet, boasting how he could still hunt. I was bursting with happiness, of course. But I should have known better. He wouldn't talk to Dibinarra about anything serious. Or to Yilimarra. Just said he was having his holiday, his walkabout. Dibinarra had to quieten Yilimarra down. 'Just let him settle,' he reckoned. 'Let him settle.' But Jandamarra was never the 'settling' type.

The howl of a dingo. JANDAMARRA *howls, long and low, answering the call.*

Night. WANGAMARRA *starts a wangga song, a slow solo, which he accompanies with a steady clapstick beat, and then a dijeridoo played by* MARRALAM. *The* BUNUBA *join* JINI *on stage, and the wangga begins. Turn and turn about, pairs of men dance extravagantly.* JINI *signals* MARRALAM's *wife* WIYALA *to join her in the women's dance, swaying in counterpoint to the men.*

JANDAMARRA *arrives, to cheers and backslapping, and joins in the dancing.*

As the cycle of song, then dance is repeated, the dancing becomes more extravagant, and the calls from the watchers get louder. And with each stanza JANDAMARRA *flirts more brazenly with a responsive* WIYALA, *even as she stands, swaying, next to* JINI.

MARRALAM *can be seen getting agitated, until eventually he throws down his dijeridoo, moves across, grabs* WIYALA *by an arm, and with an angry gesture for* JANDAMARRA, *leads her off.*

The wangga breaks up, and all except JANDAMARRA *drift off. He watches* WIYALA *leave. They exchange a look and she is gone. He follows, smiling.*

SCENE NINETEEN

Bush camp, morning. JANDAMARRA *runs back on, grinning broadly, and sprawls out to sleep with a satisfied air.* DIBINARRA *and* JINI *stroll on.*

DIBINARRA: [*amused*] Nguja bagarangarri gawarra rawurra nhi malngarri.ingga binarri.ama. [*He's still sleeping and the sun is high. The whitefellers must've taught him that style.*]

JINI: Yiningga gima thayjinyuwa. Nyirrami yani gigawudigi nhi nguja bagara. [*He does that at the station. All the others are up while he's still sleeping.*]

They try unsuccessfully to wake him. MARRALAM *charges in with* ILAJI *on his heels, both brandishing spears.*

MARRALAM: [*furious*] **Ngarragi-ngarri wiyi bagaya.** Linggawunbirrantha. [*You slept with my wife. Just you wait.*]

JANDAMARRA *gets to his feet as* YILIMARRA *comes running. He snatches up his own spear and faces* MARRALAM *defiantly.*

Nginyji tharrajangi. Ngindaji jinali nganggu. [*You're a dog. This spear is for you.*]

MARRALAM *lunges at* JANDAMARRA, *but* DIBINARRA *steps between them. There is a short, tense stand-off.*

JANDAMARRA: [*defiantly*] Yudba Marralam. **Ngunda-ingga yurawunggunu.** [*I'm not frightened of you, Marralam.*]

MARRALAM: Dabaama Ilaji! [*Grab him, Ilaji!*]

ILAJI *lunges,* JANDAMARRA *whirls, and their spears clash.*

DIBINARRA: [*commandingly*] Nguja. [*Wait.*]

He faces MARRALAM, *placing his hands on his shoulders.*

[*Quietly*] Wila lawirra? [*Can we talk?*]

MARRALAM *can't contain himself.*

MARRALAM: [*to* DIBINARRA, *snarling*] Nginyji-ingga jimiy yaarri-ingga gurrijbarra; bilih wadbama. **Ngayi walalayini nyanangarri.u.** [*You tell us to look after him; it's bullshit. He doesn't respect anybody.*]

DIBINARRA *gently pushes* MARRALAM *away.* ILAJI *stays nearby with spear poised.* DARRUDI *joins him.*

ILAJI: Gunda ngarragi! [*My own cousin brother!*]

DARRUDI: Nginyjagawu Jandamarra? [*Why, Jandamarra?*]

JANDAMARRA *ignores them both. He calmly lays down his spear and sits.* JINI *looks at him with disbelief.*

JINI: **Malngarri jangi banganggayali. Nganyi jimi, yaningi ngayini jirrmalanda.** [*You've come back like a white man. What you did brings shame on me.*]

He just keeps eating.

Milawa Yilimarra. Nganyi bilimi? [*Look at him, Yilimarra! What should I do?*]

DIBINARRA *and* MARRALAM *return.* YILIMARRA *gestures* JINI *to be quiet.* DIBINARRA *waits for* JANDAMARRA *to look, to stand up, but he does not.*

DIBINARRA: **Nyagawunggunu jinali-ngarri bidi-yuwa, milu bujawuni. [*Let him spear your leg, and the trouble will be finished.*]**

JANDAMARRA *makes them wait. Eventually he gets to his feet.*

JANDAMARRA: Ngayini ngayi wadgungura. [*No. I'm not going to.*]

DIBINARRA *throws out an arm to keep* MARRALAM *back.*

DIBINARRA: **Buga ngayi yathanggurangu wadbira. [*You can't stay here then, my nephew. You'll have to leave.*]**

JANDAMARRA *holds* DIBINARRA'*s eye defiantly. He takes his spear, turns on his heel and walks away without a backward glance, even for a distraught* JINI.

WANGAMARRA: [*sung*] Yali wali ngaya ba mindi yadi
Yali wali ngaya ba mindi yadi

SCENE TWENTY

The singing carries over. JANDAMARRA *appears alone, high on the range in evening light. He stabs at something with his spear and gets up, holding a snake. Arms outstretched, holding the python, its neck in one hand, and tail in the other, he is almost dancing as he weaves forward, seeming to make the snake slither through the air. The singing stops.*

JANDAMARRA: [*singsong*] Buwunungu… bagari gawarra-yuwa… Wadbanginyma. [*Python… sleeping in the sun… I got you.*] **Bilirri nganggi urugawuwila… Guju nganggi udgalha! [*I will take your spirit! Your bones will be lost!*]**

He turns the snake's head to face him.

That's what Yilimbirri Unggud been tell me. Are you a talking snake like him?… You got anything to say to me?

He stands straighter and gives the snake a shake.

Ngandi ngabila nganggi, guju garrawularri winthali-yuwa. [*I will eat your flesh, and burn your bones.*]

He throws it over his shoulder and exits. Lights down. Night sounds.

SCENE TWENTY-ONE

RICHARDSON *is cleaning a rifle. He aims, fires, shakes his head.*

RICHARDSON: Damn. [*He tries again.*] Little bit left and high still.

JANDAMARRA *enters, putting his shirt on.*

Well, I'll be buggered. Look who's here! Joe coughed up for a couple of new rifles. Here.

He tosses the rifle to JANDAMARRA *who hefts it to his shoulder.*

So how was life back in the Stone Age?

JANDAMARRA: [*pointing*] Bottom boab nut. See 'im?

RICHARDSON: [*doubtfully*] Yeah.

JANDAMARRA *swings the rifle to his shoulder, aims quickly, fires.* RICHARDSON *looks at him in awe. As he hands the rifle back:*

JANDAMARRA: Damn 'em. I'll stick with you, Earl.

RICHARDSON: That's my boy. [*A sudden thought*] Down on your knees, Pigeon.

JANDAMARRA: [*puzzled, and suspicious*] What?

RICHARDSON: Down on your knees I said.

Grinning all the while, he manoeuvers JANDAMARRA *onto his knees.*

No, not like that, one foot out.

He manages to get JANDAMARRA *to a position where he is kneeling on one knee in front of him. He draws a knife from his belt.* MAYANNIE *has emerged and is looking alarmed.*

I, William Richardson, Earl of Lillimooloora, by the power vested in me by King Joseph of Brooking, hereby dub thee Sir Pigeon, to be my most trusted equerry and companion. Arise, Sir Pigeon!

JANDAMARRA: [*getting to his feet, and throwing* MAYANNIE *an 'is he alright?' look*] You still on the grog, Bill?

RICHARDSON: [*laughing*] I wish, Pigeon.

He throws an arm around him.

The first black knight of the Kimberley.

He leads JANDAMARRA *and* MAYANNIE *off.*

SCENE TWENTY-TWO

Projected animation #11: Fire animation `

YILIMARRA *and* MARRALAM *watch from the range. They grin as* ILAJI *and* DARRUDI *run on with flaming torches, bending as they run to touch the torches to the ground. Smoke billows and the set is lit up with the glow of flames.*

MARRALAM: We decided it was time to strike back. The plains burned that dry season like never before, and every lungful of smoke I breathed made me feel stronger. From Gurang.ngadja to Limalurru, we left their sheep and cattle with nothing to eat but ashes. I would look down and see Jandamarra with that white bastard as they rode from fire to fire, trying to rescue those stupid sheep, and I would grip my spear tighter and think, 'One day, one day'.

SCENE TWENTY-THREE

The glow of flames is still flickering as JOE *sits at Lillimooloora.* RICHARDSON *approaches wiping his brow, exhausted.*

RICHARDSON: When d'you get here?
JOE: Couple of hours back. The Ten Mile Paddock's gone up by the look of it?
RICHARDSON: Sheep carcasses everywhere, boss. Can't get the smell of burnt wool out of me nostrils. It's a bloody disaster.
JOE: They'll pay, the bastards. They'll pay.

He opens a rum bottle and passes it to RICHARDSON.

Had a council of war in Derby. Me'n Forrest and the coppers. You're going to be out of a job shortly.
RICHARDSON: What the hell! Is that the thanks I get for bustin' me arse like this?
JOE: Wool prices are down, and there's new beef markets opening up in the goldfields. We're going to concentrate on building up the cattle side at Brooking.
RICHARDSON: [*surprised*] What? Just walk away? Leave your son's grave to the blackfellers?

JOE: There's the twist. Forrest's wrangled the money for some new police stations, and we're going to lease this place out to 'em. Lindsay's going to have a police guard.

RICHARDSON: I'll be buggered.

JOE: Only thing is, a police station's not much chop without policemen, is it? And every bushman in the colony seems to be heading for Coolgardie with bloody gold fever.

RICHARDSON: I might have to join 'em.

JOE: Maybe not. There's no time to waste training up some twerp fresh off a boat from London. Me and Forrest want action. You can expect a visit from Inspector Drewry in the not too distant future. And he just might have an interesting offer for you, if you get my drift.

RICHARDSON *takes the bottle and raises it to* JOE, *laughing.*

SCENE TWENTY-FOUR

JINI: They reckon Richardson told that police boss he'd only take the job if he could have Jandamarra for his tracker. When they told me that they were wearing police uniforms, I wouldn't believe it at first. But Dibinarra's sister-in-law saw it with her own eye, those two riding into her camp at dawn, guns firing. Nobody was killed, but most of her mob were taken away on the chain. By my own son. My own son. There were more raids. Up and down our country, people were taken away. Everybody was looking at me sideways. If it wasn't for my brother Dibinarra standing up for me, I would have had to creep away from my own country.

SCENE TWENTY-FIVE

Bush. RICHARDSON, *looking seedy, takes a swig from a bottle as* JANDAMARRA *enters. Both are in police uniforms.*

RICHARDSON: Hair o' the dog. God, I needed that.

JANDAMARRA: Horses are saddled. Ready when you are, Earl.

RICHARDSON: No rush, cobber, siddown.

JANDAMARRA: Mayannie'll be having that baby any day now, hey?

RICHARDSON: [*ignoring this*] Gawd, they were all over me at the pub last night. Didn't have to buy a single round meself. There's nothing they like better than seeing a long line of blackfellers being delivered on the chain. One old timer reckoned we're a better outfit than Lawrence and Mingo Mick when they were clearing out the Pilbara country.

JANDAMARRA: Mingo Mick, hey? I seen him once.

RICHARDSON: They reckon he's quit the force and gone walkabout again.

He passes JANDAMARRA *the bottle. He regards it suspiciously before taking a cautious first sip.*

They don't know what to make of me, those townies. I let 'em know we're a team. 'Like bastard brothers', I told 'em. They don't get it, do they? We make our own rules out here.

JANDAMARRA *takes a slug, then hands the bottle back.*

JANDAMARRA: [*quietly*] Jangala.

RICHARDSON: What?

JANDAMARRA: Jangala. That's my skin. If we two are brothers—bastard brothers—that means you're a Jangala too.

RICHARDSON: [*laughing*] Jungle men. That's us.

JANDAMARRA: Jangala. That's my skin. Jandamarra. That's my name. My proper name.

RICHARDSON *looks at him, then shakes his head.*

RICHARDSON: Pigeon'll do me just fine, brother. Come on.

JANDAMARRA *is slow to follow him.*

SCENE TWENTY-SIX

Bush. YILIMARRA *and* DARRUDI *walk on, carrying hunting spears.*

YILIMARRA: [*pointing*] Ngurru milawa rarrgi. [*See that hill there.*]
DARRUDI: Milala nyirraji. [*I see it.*]
YILIMARRA: Balararaway Yilimbirri Unggud bagara ngarranggani. [*Balarara and Yilimbirri Unggud stopped there in the dreamtime.*]

A rifle shot rings out and DARRUDI *goes down with a piercing cry.* YILIMARRA *goes to him, then turns, spear poised, to see* JANDAMARRA. RICHARDSON *charges on, his rifle aimed.* YILIMARRA *ducks as another shot is fired, then bounds into the ranges and disappears.*

RICHARDSON: Come on, Pigeon!

RICHARDSON *runs off, chasing* YILIMARRA, *as* JANDAMARRA *frantically, helplessly, tries to comfort* DARRUDI *who is writhing in agony on the ground, sobbing against the pain as he holds his guts.* JANDAMARRA *kneels down and* DARRUDI *grasps his arm.*

DARRUDI: Jandamarra. Milawina. **Nginyjingga banggayinda.** [*Jandamarra. Look at me. You've shot me.*]

JANDAMARRA: Nyirraji.ingga. [*It was him.*]

DARRUDI: **Gunda duluggawilarri-yarra.** [*Cousin, I'm going to die.*]

JANDAMARRA: Linggawura Darrudi. Jalangurru anu. [*Just wait, Darrudi. You'll be alright.*]

RICHARDSON *emerges from the ranges, panting. As he talks,* DARRUDI, *in his death throes, lunges at him and* JANDAMARRA *has to restrain him.*

RICHARDSON: Lost him. It was Ellemara, wasn't it? Why the hell didn't you back me up? Come on, we'll pick up his tracks.

JANDAMARRA: No chance up in those rocks.

RICHARDSON: Damn! We'll double back, and we'll get him on the other side.

JANDAMARRA: [*looking at* DARRUDI] What about him?

RICHARDSON: He's too far gone. Leave him.

RICHARDSON *runs off.* JANDAMARRA *gets to his feet heavily, shaking himself free of his cousin's grasp. He picks up his rifle, aims.*

DARRUDI: [*screaming*] Jandamarraaaaa!

JANDAMARRA *flinches as he fires. He shakes, murmuring Darrudi's name, as the shot echoes.*

SCENE TWENTY-SEVEN

Bush. YILIMARRA, DIBINARRA, MARRALAM *and* ILAJI *are in a tense council.*

DIBINARRA: **Nhi-ingga thirrili gurrijga.** [*He's got power.*]

ILAJI: **Ay, nyirraji jilamana.** [*Yeah, it's called a gun.*]

DIBINARRA: [*sharply*] Ngayi yiningga. **Yilimbirri Unggud wulawunu.** [*You know what I mean. Yilimbirri Unggud spoke to him.*]

YILIMARRA: Girrgarayanbinigu juralinhi. [*And he's been running away from us since.*] [*With quiet certainty*] **Yaningi Jandamarra yathari limba ngarri.** [*While Jandamarra stays with the police, we've got no chance.*]

MARRALAM: **Nyirraji nganggi thangani ganday. Nyagawulini malayuwa.** [*This idea of yours is crazy. I should just spear him in the guts.*]

ILAJI: Marralam mindija wululara. **Gundawayi nhir banggalha,** jimarriway wadbirrantha baruduyawu. [*Marralam's right. He shot his own cousin who went through the law with him.*]

The argument continues in muted tones.

At Lillimooloora. JANDAMARRA *enters, head in hands, agitated.*

JANDAMARRA: Ie gan dil eerim orlabud, greemin naim bla mi. [*I can still hear him, screaming my name.*]

MAYANNIE *follows him on, sleeping baby in arms.*

MAYANNIE: Negsdiem mudbee Dibinarra, mudbee Jini. [*One day it's going to be Dibinarra, or Jini.*]

JANDAMARRA: [*shaking his head*] Wod Ie gudu doo? [*What should I do?*]

MAYANNIE: Leebim. Ie wunu. Ee noamor maigem mee larb longdiem nou. [*Leave him. I wish I could. He stopped making me laugh a long time ago.*]

JANDAMARRA: Wodbor yoo garn geduwai? [*Why don't you leave?*]

MAYANNIE: Ie gudu loog apda Dadee. Ee laimpela. Ie gud noa hujbin. Ie garn jus runuwai la booj gudu baibee. [*I have to look after Dad. He's lame. I've got no proper man. I can't just run off to the bush, me and the baby.*] [*Smiling*] Eneewai, mudbee yoo mied dragimub mee. [*Anyway, you'd probably track me down.*]

JANDAMARRA *stops pacing and faces* MAYANNIE.

JANDAMARRA: Ie regin. Bud nod bla im. [*I would too. But not for him.*]

They are about to embrace when the baby cries. They laugh at the untimely interruption.

Ay Jambiyindi. Nginyjagawu walang gira? [*Jambiyindi. Why are you crying?*] [*Leading* MAYANNIE *off*] Come on.

DIBINARRA *has been, pacing, thinking. He stops in front of the others.*

DIBINARRA: **Thirril-anyii gurrijga. Nyirrami-yani rirrawuwinmagi.**
[*He's got a power. Others are drawn towards him.*]

YILIMARRA *and* DIBINARRA *exchange a look.* DIBINARRA *nods.*

YILIMARRA: Barrma.nhi. **Gulawuwada. Wadbayali, nhi-ingga midgawanmagi.** [*We have to force his hand. Let's test him. Let him come and chain us up.*]

ILAJI: Yuwai.

All except MARRALAM *exit.*

MARRALAM: We were in trouble by then. Yilimarra was right about that. There was a mob of cattle coming out from Derby, and they were going to push 'em through Bandilngan, Windjana Gorge and start up a new station north of the ranges. That would've left us with nothing. So many men were in jail—put there by Jandamarra, mind you—we didn't have enough to try to stop them. Yilimarra and Dibinarra were so calm about it. They believed in Jandamarra's power, and they believed he would listen. I reckoned they were crazy, all his life he'd brought us nothing but trouble. I hated him more than I hated the whitefellers. But I went along with it. I just couldn't walk away from them. We wouldn't let Dibinarra go on the chain. He had to carry the songs and the law if it went wrong. Him and Jini went up to our lookout in the cliffs above Limalurru. We sent the rest of the women and the kids north. And we let ourselves be caught.

The BUNUBA MEN *are up high, sitting in a row, cross-legged. They begin to sing.* MARRALAM *joins them, sitting at the end of the row.*

BUNUBA MEN: [*sung*] Limalurru dawulma biyinggidi, Limalurru
          dawulma biyinggidi
          Galanganyja dawulma biyinggidi, Galanganyja dawulma
          biyinggidi.
          Limalurru dawulma biyinggidi, Limalurru dawulma
          biyinggidi
          Galanganyja dawulma biyinggidi, Galanganyja dawulma
          biyinggidi.

The sound swells.

JANDAMARRA *and* RICHARDSON *discover the singing* MEN. *The singing does not falter, and the* MEN *keep looking straight down.*

RICHARDSON: [*threatening* YILIMARRA *with his rifle, shouting*] Don't move! Don't move, or I'll blow your head off!

He paces up and down the line of MEN, *continuing to mutter threats, looking as if he is about to shoot. The* MEN *do not flinch. The singing does not stop. If anything, it grows louder.* JANDAMARRA *is aware something is wrong, as he places a loop of chain around the neck of each singing* MAN. *The chaining complete, he steps back.*

Get up! Get up!… I'll blow your head off! Get up!

The singing does not stop, the MEN *do not move, until:*

JANDAMARRA: Get up.

Immediately the MEN *rise, still singing. They ignore* RICHARDSON's *order to move, only doing so when* JANDAMARRA *speaks.* RICHARDSON *leads the singing chain gang on a slow circuit of the stage, walking the 'turkey trot' towards the station.* JANDAMARRA *trails nervously, spooked.*

Eventually they reach Lillimooloora. Again they ignore RICHARDSON's *orders as he tries to make them sit. They only respond to* JANDAMARRA. *Finally seated, still the* MEN *sing.*

RICHARDSON: Shut up! Shut up!

He turns away, and sees JANDAMARRA *watching.*

What's wrong with you, cobber? Ellemara himself, and every other bastard on the most wanted list. We'll be in the Perth papers—the toast of Western Australia. Come on.

He heads over to the house as MAYANNIE *enters.* JANDAMARRA *remains, held by the eyes of* YILIMARRA. *All the* OTHERS, *also staring at him, keep singing.*

YILIMARRA's *gesture is awkward, but clear: hands spread, a palms-up gesture, offering himself and the others up to* JANDAMARRA.

MAYANNIE *offers the singing* PRISONERS *water, one by one. While she does this,* RICHARDSON *re-enters, bottle in hand.*

Have a drink, Pigeon. We deserve it.

JANDAMARRA: [*uneasily, ignoring the proffered bottle*] Something's wrong. We didn't see any women or kids on the whole damned patrol.

RICHARDSON: All the better. It's the bucks we want, isn't it? This is our day, brother. Once we've got 'em into Derby I might take me leave. Go down to Perth and get drunk for a month. Maybe I'll sell me story to one of the rags down there. What next? That's the question! What next for the brothers in bastardry?

Carried away in his drunken excitement, RICHARDSON *charges off again.* JANDAMARRA *can't escape the pressure of the voices. He hides his head in his hands and sinks to the floor. The singing continues, until* MAYANNIE *steps forward and speaks above it.*

MAYANNIE: It went on for days. Jandamarra hardly said a word, but his nightmares made him scream.

JANDAMARRA *starts to his feet, tears off his police jacket, and paces, as* MAYANNIE *once again offers the* PRISONERS *water. This time they drink, but the singing does not stop.*

RICHARDSON *re-enters. He gives* MAYANNIE *a sour look, takes a slug, then waves the bottle at* JANDAMARRA.

RICHARDSON: Want some?

He suddenly charges at MAYANNIE.

Piss off out of it! Or I'll blow your head off!

He chases her offstage, rifle pointed. He takes another slug, then throws the bottle away. He glares at the singing men.

You know what?... I should put a bullet in that Ellemara right now. S'worth 50 quid from ol' Bligh—no questions asked. Bugger all the problems of getting him to Derby in one piece.

He approaches them, rifle poised. He staggers. Points again. Yawns drunkenly. He lays down, still glaring at the PRISONERS. *But his head drops. He falls into a drunken sleep.*

MAYANNIE *enters. She sits nearby, cross-legged, and joins the singing, clapping the relentless beat.*

JANDAMARRA *watches for a few moments, taking all this in. He approaches the sleeping* RICHARDSON *and gently eases the rifle away from him.*

He steps back. Aims at RICHARDSON. *Steps closer. Lowers the rifle. Paces.*

As one, the PRISONERS *look up at him, and the intensity of the singing picks up, as their eyes bore into him.*

He turns. Now he is standing over RICHARDSON, *rifle aimed.*

JANDAMARRA: [*softly*] Earl… Jangala.

RICHARDSON *looks up.*

Rifle shot!

RICHARDSON *falls back. Dead.*

The singing stops.

The shot echoes. The cockatoos screech.

MAYANNIE *and the* MEN *do not move as* JANDAMARRA *runs off. The lights fade to blackout.*

END OF ACT ONE

ACT TWO

SCENE TWENTY-EIGHT

Transformation music as the lights come up and MARRALAM *and* JINI *enter from opposite sides.*

MARRALAM: Dibinarra and Jini were hiding high up there in the ranges, waiting. Then Jini heard the shot.

The rifle shot is heard again.

JINI: I held my breath. Then I heard Ilaji and the others cheering.

The sound of cheers.

I knew my boy had come back to us. I skipped down those rocks like a nanny goat, like a little girl, just running to get there.

MARRALAM: But he was gone. Took off without a word. He left Mayannie to unlock us all. None of us knew what would happen. What to do.

JINI: When he walked in next morning, he said to dig a grave for Richardson. And then he just sat there, cleaning his rifle.

Lights up on JANDAMARRA *at Lillimooloora, cleaning a rifle, as around him, the* BUNUBA *come and go in high spirits, carting goods, trashing and deconstructing the homestead.* YILIMARRA *watches* JANDAMARRA.

ILAJI *emerges wielding a cut-throat razor.*

ILAJI: Nginyjaga ngindaji? [*What's this?*]

JANDAMARRA *ignores him.* ILAJI *snaps the razor shut without meaning to, cutting himself in the process. He exclaims and sucks at a finger.*

YILIMARRA *calls the hijinks to a halt and turns to* JANDAMARRA.

YILIMARRA: **Ngayi ban.ganggurangi. Nginyji-ingga banggayiya limba.** [*You can't go back now. You've shot a policeman.*]

JANDAMARRA: Ganday bagaray, jimarri-ngarragi nyirraji. [*He was a rough bastard, but he was my friend.*] Like Lindsay Bligh was. My two mates are finished. **N̲ginyji ga̲n.bawuwinanyi dulug'gaanju.** [*If you follow me, you might die too.*]

MARRALAM *joins them as* YILIMARRA *answers.*

YILIMARRA: **N̲gayini garrganybu.** [*I can't leave you.*]

MARRALAM: **Nhi ga̲ninyi ma yathari?** [*He's in charge now, is he?*]

JA̲NDAMARRA: **Ma̲lngarri-i̲ngga muway ba̲na̲nggarrwanbinigi... N̲gindaji gurrijgurragi.** [*Whitefellers are coming to take our country. They'll have these.*] [*Getting to his feet*] Jilamana, bulit, ganpowda. **Armi ja̲ngi.** [*They've got guns, bullets, gunpowder. Just like an army.*]

ILAJI *has rejoined them now.*

ILAJI: **N̲ginyjaga armi?** [*What's an army?*]

JA̲NDAMARRA: **Nyana-n̲garri gurama jilamana n̲garri.** [*A big mob of men with guns.*]

Silence until MAYANNIE enters, with the baby crying.

JA̲NDAMARRA *turns to* MAYANNIE *and the babe, as* JINI *joins them.*

Borbela Jambiyindi, yoo gudim noa Dadee nou. [*Poor feller Jambiyindi. You've got no father now.*]

[*Taking the swaddled babe*] Mie boi. [*My son.*]

MAYANNIE *throws her arms around him. He kisses the babe then passes him back to her. He picks up his rifle and leads everyone off.*

Ba wadbarra.

SCENE TWENTY-NINE

The lowing of a big herd of cattle is heard. JA̲NDAMARRA, MAYANNIE, YILIMARRA *and* ILAJI *take position on vantage points in the ranges, guns at the ready.* MARRALAM *runs on.*

MARRALAM: Wadgurragali. [*They're coming.*]

JA̲NDAMARRA *aims and fires. His rifle shot rings out.*

JA̲NDAMARRA *remains frozen in the firing position, watching, as the others show themselves.*

ILAJI: Nyirrami girrgarami. [*The other one's getting away.*]

He shoots inexpertly. The recoil sends him stumbling backwards.

Aah, nginyjaga.nhi. [Aah, shit!]

The shot seems to bring JANDAMARRA *back to reality. He glares at* ILAJI, *kneels, aims, fires, immediately followed by* MAYANNIE *with her rifle.*

Yaiyee! **Duluggawuwurranintha!** [*Both of them dead!*]

MARRALAM *enters, dragging* GEORGIE, *an Aboriginal stockman who throws himself to the ground. With his hands up, he pleads for his life.*

JANDAMARRA: [*calling*] Jorjee! Gidub! [*Georgie! Get up!*]

GEORGIE *rolls onto his back, in a state of terror as he eyes* JANDAMARRA.

Gidub Ie bin sai. [*Get up I said.*]

GEORGIE *struggles to his feet, shaking with fright.* JANDAMARRA *looks around at the others to make sure they get the message.*

Jorjee, dulim orlu thaijin mob, en bileej mob, orl lud. **Wee gudim bag ou gundree nou. Enee wujbulu wee fiendim lu Bunuba gundree na, wee guddu gillim.** Yoo gibidim thud wird. [*Georgie, you tell all the station mob, all the police mob, everybody. We're taking our country back now. Any whitefeller we find on Bunuba land now, we kill them. You tell them that.*]

GEORGIE: [*retreating*] Yij boj. Janggiyoo, janggiyoo. Ul dulim orlabud Bijin. [*Yes, boss. Thank you, thank you. I'll tell them, Pigeon.*]

JANDAMARRA: Oi Jorjee!

GEORGIE *turns.*

[*Laughing*] Mudbee thai guddu jidim julb? Liegu yoo. [*Reckon they'll shit 'emselves? Like you.*]

A shot from MARRALAM *near his feet makes* GEORGIE *skip as he rushes off.*

Ba wadbarra, waginyawu! [*Come on. Don't let that wagon get away!*]

JANDAMARRA *runs off, followed by all except* MARRALAM.

MARRALAM: What a feast we had that night! We cut the fattest cows out of that big herd, and got all sorts of fancy tucker out of the wagon. Jandamarra was right about the guns too. He started teaching us how to use them. He had a plan, and by then, as far as fighting the whitefellers went, I was ready to do whatever he said. Dibinarra wasn't happy. He'd been to Yilimbirri's spring. The water there was gandayi—no good. He reckoned that Yillimbirri Unggud snake wasn't looking after his country. He said we had to go and sing for the snake. But Jandamarra said, 'I'm here to fight. Not to sing the snake.' He wouldn't go anywhere near Yilimbirri.

SCENE THIRTY

ILAJI *enters wearing a silly wig and a robe, followed by* FORREST. *Other actors don silly hats and become* MPs *making parliamentary-style interjections.*

ILAJI: [*shouting*] Order! Order in the House! The Member for the Kimberley has the floor!

FORREST: Mr Speaker, Honourable Members, the treacherous attack at Devil's Pass cost not only the lives of Burke and Gibbs—

Angry interjections.

—and the loss of many hundreds of stock. On top of their arsenal from Lillimooloora, the murderers seized—let me list it—one Winchester rifle, one Schneider rifle, a double-barrelled shotgun and four revolvers! 4,000 rounds of ammunition, four pounds of gunpowder and 20 pounds of shot.

MEMBERS *are shocked.*

Gentlemen, we are facing an insurrection! In these circumstances, I must ask of you, is the life of one white man not worth that of a thousand natives?

The sound of morse code. The CROWD *yells its agreement as they transform into Derby townsfolk and become* JOE's CROWD *in Derby.*

JOE *enters, waving a piece of paper, and holds up his hands for silence.* MARY *follows him and watches.*

JOE: Good people of Derby, 'Is the life of one white man not worth that of a thousand natives!' That was Forrest in the Parliament in Perth last night. And there's not a true white man in this land would say otherwise!

The CROWD *cheers.*

There's already three white men dead out there. And Edgar only escaped by the skin of his teeth. You can do your sums as well as me! I fed and I clothed that heathen devil Pigeon when he was a young'un. And against my better judgement I let him back to work on Lilli-mooloora. Richardson—may he rest in peace—called him a brother! Enough of trust. Enough of charity. Let our bullets do the talking!

A frenzy of cheering as JOE *flourishes the piece of paper with one hand and hefts a rifle with the other. The* CROWD *fades away as* MARY *runs to* JOE.

MARY: Joe, this is about Lindsay, isn't it? He wouldn't want you to have blood on your hands.

JOE: 'Blood on my hands.' How dare you! You think *my* son would've stood by and let these savages wreak their havoc?! They'll have gobbled up Burke and Gibbs' kidney fat by now. And you know what? The devils will've dug up Lindsay's bones by now, to use in their cursed potions.

He brandishes his hands at her, shouting as he exits.

Let 'em be covered in blood. The more the better. As long as it's nigger blood.

MARY: And so the madness began.

SCENE THIRTY-ONE

JINI *enters. There are night sounds as she closes her eyes, gathering her memories, before launching into the story.* OTHERS *re-enact the story, making grass bundles, etc.* JA<u>ND</u>AMARRA *can be seen directing the* OTHERS.

JINI: We knew what they were going to do; the police always came at first light.

MAYANNIE: There was no moon—that was good for us. We used all the blankets from Limalurru to cover up bundles of grass—make it look like there was a mob camping down by the river. Jandamarra picked out the places for the all the men with guns, and gave them their orders.

JINI: I was in the back of the big cave, in charge of all the women and kids. Not Mayannie though.

JOE, BARNETT *and* TROOPERS *creep on and take up positions.*

MAYANNIE: They came creeping in, just like he said. Two lots, one from the north end, one from the south. They settled down, watching our ghost camp. And we watched them. All waiting for the dawn.

JINI: We knew as soon as he fired the first shot, all the others would follow. If they shot straight, most of those police would be dead before they knew it. The police, the station mob, Joe Bligh. The whole lot… It was that blacktracker Jim Crowe that saved them, coming down over the top with those Queensland boys.

JIM CROWE: [*offstage, shouting*] Take cover! They're in the rocks!

The sound of one shot.

JINI: His shot put a hole in the sergeant's hat, but not in his head. That's how close it was. After that it was like…

MAYANNIE: Like hell. Everybody shooting. The sounds bouncing around off the walls of the gorge. All the white cockies screeching, the kids screaming and crying.

A fusilade, actors ducking and shooting. The screeching of cocka-toos, screaming and gunshots.

But then it just stopped… Everybody was just shooting at shadows. The malngarri had got cover, and our mob were hidden. The bullets were just bouncing off rocks.

Lights up on JOE *and another squatter,* ALF BARNETT, *hunkered down.*

JOE: Must be five hours, Alf.

BARNETT: She's a stalemate alright. First one on either side makes a move is gonna get his head blown off.

JOE: Least we've got shade. It'll be getting hot for the coppers over there.

BARNETT: Reckon it was only Phillips got hit?

BARNETT *cautiously raises his head to peer out.*

JOE: Think so.

Bang! BARNETT *ducks back down.*

JANDAMARRA: [*calling*] **Ngayi bujawunggurrugu bulit. Yarri Bunuba. Yarri linggawarra.** [*Don't waste your bullets. We're Bunuba. We know how to wait.*]

MAYANNIE: Yilimarra must've had something he needed to tell Jandamarra.

YILIMARRA *is on the move. The boom of a shotgun. He clutches at his back and goes down.*

JOE: Got the bastard!

There is an outbreak of cheering and a fusilade of shots. JANDAMARRA *appears.*

JINI: Jandamarra ran out to drag him in, but Yilimarra waved him back— he knew he was gone. That's when Jandamarra took his first bullet.

We see this.

He didn't feel it. He was just staring at Yilimarra, crying.

She pauses. She shudders before picking up the story again.

The police got a better line on the cave, and the bullets started coming inside. A woman and two kids were hurt. And he just stood there. Then they were charging across the sand, to get up close.

MAYANNIE: [*screaming*] Jandamarraa!

JINI: He stepped out, and let off two shots. Then he took his next bullet.

JANDAMARRA *staggers.*

MARRALAM: Us men in the other caves ran out of bullets. Soon it was just Jandamarra and Ilaji left, with Mayannie reloading the guns for them.

JINI: I started pushing all the women and kids back up the tunnel. It was a nightmare. Climbing through all these rough, tiny tunnels. Everyone crying, scared. But they got through, up to the top and clear away.

JANDAMARRA'*s actions match* JINI'*s description.* MAYANNIE *can be seen passing rifles to him and* ILAJI, *letting off a couple of shots.*

MAYANNIE: Jandamarra took another bullet, through his shoulder. I was screaming at him to pull out, but he was telling me to hold on, so the others could get a start.

JINI: He was at the front of the cave—three bullets he had already—and he leaned against the rock with one hand—all bloody it was—and he kept firing and firing. He was hit in the leg. Another one in the guts, and still he didn't stop. Till at last he collapsed, and slid down. He left this big bloody scrape on the rock.

MAYANNIE: [*screaming*] Waaraa! **Ngay wadbayurrmagi!** [***Don't let them take him!***]

> MAYANNIE *and* ILAJI *drag* JANDAMARRA *back and they disappear.* ILAJI *reappears and pops off one last shot. The wailing of women can be heard over* JINI*'s lines and into the start of the next scene.*

JINI: We thought he was dead. It was like a dream, but somehow we got him through that tunnel, up to the top of the cliff, and away to Tunnel Creek.

> *Over* JINI*'s last lines,* JOE *leads* BARNETT *and a* TROOPER *up. They peer into the cave, whilst* JOE *scrapes the rock with a finger, which he then licks.*

SCENE THIRTY-TWO

The next day, at Lillimooloora. JOE *is kneeling by Lindsay's grave, carefully wrapping a canvas parcel.* BARNETT *and a* TROOPER *enter.*

BARNETT: [*calling anxiously*] Joe?! You coming?! [*To himself*] What's he doing?

TROOPER: Did you see him back there, Mr Barnett? Dipping his finger in that pool of Pigeon's blood? Tasting it? [*Shaking his head*] I reckon he's losing the plot.

BARNETT: Leave him be.

TROOPER: I'm more than happy to stay out of his way.

> JOE *gets to his feet, holding the canvas parcel. He looks around, before he lets his gaze come to rest on the* TROOPER.

JOE: We gave this place to you lot. Look at it. Wrecked.

BARNETT: Come on, Joe, we've got to hit the track.

> JOE *ignores the* TROOPER, *addressing himself to* BARNETT, *who has looked across to the grave, then back to* JOE.

JOE: I'll not abandon my son.

BARNETT: Jesus, Joe!

JOE: I'll not abandon him to them, I tell you! I was going to get him away from here. Down to school. He'd've come back a man, and we'd've taken on the world. I was going to get him away.

He sits, the parcel on his knees.

Better late than never, hey boy. It's no fit place this. Not now.

The TROOPER *steps back, appalled.* BARNETT *squats beside* JOE.

BARNETT: Joe, we've got to go. Come on. This is no time to be riding solo.

JOE: You go. I'll follow directly.

The TROOPER *and* BARNETT *exit as* JOE *tenderly brushes dirt from the canvas, then hugs the parcel to his chest.*

Flesh of my flesh. There's naught but bones now.

He stumbles to his feet and walks unheedingly across stage, talking to the canvas parcel.

They killed you, Lindsay, sure as he killed that fool Richardson and the others with his bullets. I know it. They'll not take you for their wicked spells, lad.

He turns and crosses back.

In holy ground you'll rest. White man's ground.

MAYANNIE *and* ILAJI *drag/carry a desperately wounded* JANDAMARRA *to his recovery place. She arranges his head on her lap and sits stroking him.*

SCENE THIRTY-THREE

The lights change. Derby. MARY *storms on as* JOE *approaches, still staring down at the parcel of bones.*

MARY: How *dare* you!

JOE: I saved him from them, Mary.

MARY: From who?! From what?!

JOE: We must see to his funeral.

MARY: We! This is your... [*searching for the word*] ... crusade. Not mine. I'll have none of it, Joe. [*Defiantly*] I'm going back to the station.

JOE: Fine. Just don't expect me back there for a good while yet. I will bury my son—in holy ground. And then there is a job to be done. I'll crush those vermin.

MARY: What is happening to you? Lindsay loved that land. He was happy there like no other place in his short life... You had no right to move him. No right. He was my son too, Joe.

MARY *runs off as* FORREST *enters.*

FORREST: They're finally getting serious down in Perth. They're sending Sergeant Lawrence up.

JOE: Lawrence, hey? They say he's done a good job in the Pilbara.

FORREST: And his offsider, Mingo Mick. And listen to his orders! [*Reading*] 'Upon arrival you are to assume control of the whole force and direction of the operations against the natives. In doing so you must be guided by circumstances and your own judgement.'

JOE: Free rein at last!

FORREST: [*reading*] 'You must understand that the object of your mission is to free the district in a decisive manner and act promptly in the matter.' It's about time, eh? There'll be extra coppers and trackers coming with him, not to mention guns and ammo. Any local who'll volunteer can be sworn in as a Special.

JOE: Special Constable Bligh reportin' for duty, Alexander. I'll give Lawrence the guided tour.

FORREST: I figured you might.

JOE *and* FORREST *exit.*

SCENE THIRTY-FOUR

Lights up on JANDAMARRA. *Still* MAYANNIE *sits stroking him as she softly sings the Dirrara lament.* MARRALAM *enters.*

MARRALAM: They started up near Garang.ngadja and came down the river. Lawrence's mob on the north side, Joe Bligh and his men on the south.

A rifle shot, offstage.

From Garang.ngadja through to Derby—200 miles... And hundreds of bodies.

MARRALAM *continues as a* WARRIOR *staggers on, holding a wound.*
He collapses. JOE *follows, then crouches over the body, cutting.*
He stands, holding a necklace of animal bones. He examines them,
fondles them, then places them around his neck.

I watched from the cliffs, talking to the ones who survived, taking word back to Dibinarra in Tunnel Creek when I could. One Noonkanbah bloke told me a bad spirit had got hold of Bligh. He rode in there from Milijidee side one night and started dragging people out of their beds, screaming at them.

JOE: [*screaming*] Where is he?! Where's Pigeon?! Tell me, or I'll take the whip to you!

JOE *staggers off, clutching at the bone necklace.* MAYANNIE's *song*
is heard again for a few more bars, then MARY *enters.*

MARY: I saw Joe once in three months. I sat it out at Brooking Springs. Long, silent days and nights, with the air hanging heavy, as if there was an evil taint to it.

MAYANNIE's *song again.* JINI *enters.*

JINI: We never thought he'd live, but Yilimbirri Unggud wouldn't let him go. Three months he was layin' there, inside Tunnel Creek, barely alive, while Lawrence and Bligh ran wild. They shot everyone they found who wasn't shivering in the station camps.

MARY: [*turning to* JINI, *shocked*] But Lawrence's report said there were twenty-eight shot.

JINI: [*furious*] Twenty-eight! Bullshit, Mary! It was everyone they found. Not just Bunuba. Gooniyandi, Nyigina, Walmajarri, Mangala, Unggumi. Ngarinyin. Everyone.

What, you reckon blackfellers can't count? Twenty-eight! I know the names of the dead. I knew the husbands and wives and grannies and little kids that got left behind.

The lament again, louder this time, MAYANNIE *crying as she sings.*
JINI *turns away from* MARY, *disgusted.*

MARRALAM: One day, I was following Lawrence and his gang. I came over the crest of the range and spotted their camp. They had five men and two women chained up round a tree. I was too far away to hear him proper, but Lawrence was shouting at the trackers. Those trackers were shaking their heads and trying to back away, but Lawrence kept at them. I saw them lift up their rifles, and I heard the shots, and the screaming of the women, until all seven of them were dead, right there on the chain. Then they took the chains off them, and piled a mob of wood around the tree, and started the fire... I could smell it, all the way up there on the range, those bodies burning.

MARY: Surely not.

> JINI *and* MARRALAM *give her scathing looks, taking a step towards her.*

> MARY *realises that they are speaking the truth and tries to take it in.*

SCENE THIRTY-FIVE

Projected animation #12: Raii flicker around JANDAMARRA.

JANDAMARRA *is alone now. Images of the Raii—the spirits of the Bunuba world—can be seen flickering around him. There is a low rumbling: the sound of Yilimbirri Unggud. He stirs slightly.*

Projected animation #13: Snake breathing, smaller in girth (further away), but bright.

The projected image of a snake appears on the rocks above JANDAMARRA. *For a moment, the rumble is louder, before fading again.* JANDAMARRA *twitches, then is suddenly awake. He sees the image of the snake and half sits, propping on his elbows.*

YILIMBIRRI UNGGUD: Iminyji.

> *The word echoes.* JANDAMARRA *sits up properly.*

Ban.gawina muway-yawu. [*Bring me home.*]

> *The rumble flares, and then fades away, as does the snake image.*

JANDAMARRA: [*fearfully*] Yilimbirri Unggud.

> *He gets gingerly to his feet. He feels his torso uncertainly, then leans for a few moments on the rocks. He takes a step back, and almost falls. Eventually, he staggers down.*

> MAYANNIE *is the first to see him. She bounds to his side to support him.* DIBINARRA, MARRALAM *and* ILAJI *run on and join them, hovering anxiously.*

Yilimbirri U_nggudingga wayami n_garragi. 'Ban.gawina muway-yawu!' [*Yillimbirri U_nggud called to me. He said, 'Bring me home'.*]

ILAJI: [*bewildered*] **N_ga nhi?** [*Where is he?*]

JA_NDAMARRA: **Iminyji-yawu. Birriga N_garinyin muwayi,** nyirrami-yuwa bi_lanyi… Iminyji-yuwa yathawurrantha. [*Iminyji. In the north-west near N_garinyin country, with the snake there… He's gone to Iminyji.*]

> JA_NDAMARRA *closes his eyes, exhausted. He leans back against* MAYANNIE, *who holds him tight and gently rocks him.*

ILAJI: [*deeply alarmed*] Yilimbirri U_nggud Iminyji yuwa? **N_ginyjaganhi warigawanu?** [*Yillimbirri U_nggud at Iminyji? Why did he leave?*]

> DIBINARRA, *though, looks as if a penny has dropped.*

DIBINARRA: **Nyirraji n_gambi milha minybali bagawurragi. Winyji n_gay.** [*That's why the meat is all skinny. Why we can't get rain.*]

ILAJI: Nhir muwayi nyirraji. N_garran_ggani nhi. [*But this is his country. From the Creation.*]

DIBINARRA: **Ma_lngarri-in_gga wirrijgiranyi garuwa.** [*It must have been when that white boy buggered up his spring.*]

> DIBINARRA *signals* ILAJI *to be quiet and gestures at* JA_NDAMARRA *who seems to have fallen asleep. They half carry him off.* MARRALAM *is left alone.*

MARRALAM: It took a clever man like Dibinarra to understand what Ja_ndamarra said; to work out what had happened. And why. All the makers of this country had their places, where they had lived since the N_garran_ggani, the Creation Time. When that friend of Ja_ndamarra's, that white boy, dug up his spring, Yilimbirri U_nggud was so angry that he left. We didn't have any stories about the U_ngguds leaving their homes. What Ja_ndamarra was telling us was unimaginable. But it rang true. That was why the country was sick. The trees were dying. The meat was skinny. And that snake calling to Ja_ndamarra, what did that mean?

SCENE THIRTY-SIX

JOE *stalks the floor, worrying at the string of bones and staring out into the darkness.*

JOE: You're out there somewhere, aren't you? Working your magic. If you were dead, I'd know it... We will meet again.

He stalks off.

SCENE THIRTY-SEVEN

Projected animation #14: Raii flicker around JANDAMARRA.

JANDAMARRA *is sitting cross-legged, where he lay in a coma. The Raii are flickering around him. He seems to be talking to them.*

JANDAMARRA: Ngalanyba!... Ngalanyba, gimangarragi. [*Sing!... Sing, sing, he keeps telling me.*] **Ngalanybila, ban.gawularri-ali. Bilirri ngarragi wurugana yarra? Mi ngarragi walay.yuwa. [*If I sing, if I bring him home, will he take my spirit? Like he told me when I was a kid.*] Nginyjaga junba ngalanybila? [*Which song will I sing?*]**

MARRALAM: Dibinarra taught Jandamarra all the law he had missed—at his initiation, and in all the years he was running with the whitefellers. That, and more. Law, and knowledge, and songs that were too deep for a man like me. Dibinarra was showing him the path to power, to becoming a Jalgangurru.

DIBINARRA: Ngarrung.ngu yathari. [*I think he is ready.*]

WANGAMARRA *sings the 'White Cockatoo' junba, which continues through this scene.*

DIBINARRA *faces* JANDAMARRA. MARRALAM *joins them. He ties bands of string around each of* JANDAMARRA*'s biceps.* DIBINARRA *puts a hand on* JANDAMARRA*'s shoulder.*

Nginyji jalgangurru thirrili ngarri. Gamanbimbirragi inya, udgawalha jirigi jangi. [*You are a medicine man, a Jalgangurru, with a big power. If they look for you, you will disappear like a bird.*]

There is just the singing, as MARRALAM *paints* JANDAMARRA *with white ochre. The painting continues, as* DIBINARRA *moves around, placing a hand on the other shoulder.*

Raii-way Yilimbirri. Nginyji-ingga yadjilinyja, nyirra jarr-way waywirrantha nganggi. Winyiwunantha. [*When Yilimbirri and the spirits call to you in your dream listen to them.*]

The singing continues as MARRALAM *carefully completes the painting, ending with the face. Then he hands an amulet of black cockatoo tail feathers to* DIBINARRA, *who places this around* JANDAMARRA*'s neck.*

[*Gesturing around them*] Milawa. Muwayi ganday bagara yaranggi. **Nginyji ganinyi wadbira muwayi jalangurru awuni… Yarri. ingga ganba.winya.** [*Look. This land is sick, Jandamarra. You must lead the way if the land is going to be healed… We will all follow you.*]

The singing ends. JANDAMARRA *dips a hand into the coolamon of ochre, then holds it high.*

MARRALAM: Jandamarra accepted his power, at last. His spirit. His bilirri. [*Pointing at the ball of* JANDAMARRA*'s thumb*] It lived here, in his hand.

JANDAMARRA *walks away from them and out of view.* 'Cooloo-coo-coor', *the cry of the topknot pigeon rings out.* MARRALAM *and* DIBINARRA *turn and watch the projection of a flying bird.*

Projected animation #15: Dub bird flies away.

SCENE THIRTY-EIGHT

JANDAMARRA *and* MAYANNIE *creep on. She scatters flour, in which he stomps, then dances before they exit.*

TRACKER GEORGIE *sees the footprints as he enters. He gasps, looks again.*

GEORGIE: Ahh, shit… Boss! Come quick!

He points urgently as a TROOPER *runs on.*

[*His voice quavering*] Look! Pigeon for track!

TROOPER: Track him down, Georgie.

GEORGIE: [*fearful*] No! He's teasing us.

TROOPER: [*raising a hand as if to give him a backhander*] I'll whip you. Track him down.

They run off, with GEORGIE *in a state of terror, as* MARY *enters.*

MARY: I had to hide the thrill I felt when I heard about the footprints in the flour at Lillimooloora. Word spread like wildfire, Pigeon was back. Joe was right.

JINI: For the next three years we were running free. They never stopped hunting us. But it was the best time for me. I had my boy back.

MAYANNIE: [*running on to join* JINI] Mostly we were just living in the old way, hunting, moving camp all the time.

JINI: It was like the days before the malngarri came.

MARY: I often used to think about Jini. Trying to imagine what her life might be like: on the run, hiding, hungry.

JINI: [*laughing*] Hungry! In our own country!

MAYANNIE: And we had fresh beef whenever we felt like it.

JINI: I wanted it to go on forever.

MAYANNIE: We could've killed plenty more whitefellers.

JINI: But Jandamarra wouldn't let us.

MAYANNIE: He'd go down and leave his tracks, or send some men down to start fires, or let themselves be seen with a gun.

JINI: But he knew if we kept killing they'd bring Lawrence back, and there would be slaughter, like it was after Bandilngan.

MAYANNIE: 'Nguja linguwurra, ngayi milu.u.' That's what he used to say. Keep them worrying, but don't make them wild.

JINI: He didn't know how to make that Unggud come home, how to clear the path for the snake. But he reckoned the best way was to make the country quiet.

MAYANNIE: And every night we sang to Yilimbirri Unggud.

MARY: By the second year me and a woman on Quanbun were the only white women left on the stations. No-one talked about anything but Pigeon. Where was he? When would they catch him? Pigeon fever, I called it.

Projected animation #16: Clouds passing quickly.

SCENE THIRTY-NINE

During the previous speeches JOE *has entered. He pulls a canvas bedroll over a body-shaped mound of brush. He picks up his rifle, retreats into the darkness, and watches.*

A mopoke's call breaks the silence. JOE *starts at a flicker of movement behind him. But before he can react,* JANDAMARRA *has an arm around his neck and a revolver held to his temple.* JANDAMARRA *takes his rifle and stands over him.*

JANDAMARRA: I know that trick, Joe Bligh. We've been watching you, riding up and down the country all on your own.

> JOE *is kneeling. There is silence, except for his raspy breath.*

I'm sick of fighting. Fighting and running. Us mob, we can only run round in circles, cos we can't leave. This is our country… You can go back, though. Where you came from. To your country.

JOE: I've got no 'country', Pigeon, none bar this.

JANDAMARRA: Stay on your side of the range, and leave us free on this side. Leave us half our country, an' maybe we can stop this war.

> JOE *laughs, bitterly, and gets to his feet.*

JOE: We're not leaving. Us whitefellers. Grass! Pasture. That's what it's about. To feed our bullocks. I need more. We all need more. But we can't do it while you're on the loose. Even if I did pack up and leave, someone'd come behind me. Not just one man either. Hundreds. Thousands. So the cards are just gonna have to fall.

> JANDAMARRA *points at* JOE's *breast, the string of bones.*

JANDAMARRA: Did you kill the man you took this from?

JOE: I rode in after Lawrence and his boys had broken up the camp. The feller was already dead. Something was telling me to take it.

> JANDAMARRA *forces* JOE *back down to his knees and takes the string.*

JANDAMARRA: That belonged to one of my uncles. I'll give it to his son, Ilaji.

JOE: I dream about you, Pigeon.

JANDAMARRA: My name is Jandamarra.

JOE: They say you're a magic man, hey… It was you witchdoctors and your magic killed Lindsay. I know it in my bones.

JANDAMARRA: What do you know about magic?

JOE: It's all about fear, I reckon. Tracker or tribesman, they're all terrified of you, aren't they, Pigeon?

JANDAMARRA: You know what magic is really?… It's power that you don't understand. I used to think guns were magic. Bang! A roo falls down dead. Or a man. But I know now… I can't make a gun. But I can make bullets. Lead from tea chests. Melt it down, shape it. Bit of gunpowder. I've got one like that in this rifle now.

> JOE *looks dubious.*

They work alright.

JOE: I'll take your word for it.

JANDAMARRA: My power comes from a place you've never been— inside my country. Not just on top, like your house. I'm talking about deep inside the land. I can go there now. I know that place. But you know what? One part of the country, he's empty. That power's gone. And that means everything is sick. No rain, you know about that, don't you, Joe Bligh? There's a reason. Ever since Lindsay went into Yilimbirri Unggud's place.

JOE: What?!

JANDAMARRA: That's what killed him. Not me, not witchdoctors. The country. The power in this country… I tried to stop Lindsay going there. I was his friend… I was too late.

> JOE *opens his mouth, but no words come.* JANDAMARRA *picks up the guns.* JOE *flinches as he approaches.*

Like I said, I'm sick of fighting. But I've got to bring that power back. Bring that Yilimbirri Unggud back home.

JOE: How?

> *Now* JANDAMARRA *is behind him again, pistol in his back.*

JANDAMARRA: I don't know yet.

JOE: [*with a strangled laugh*] Look at us, Pigeon. Both riding solo, both at our wits' end. I figured it was down to me to sort things out. So I come out into the wilderness like this to face the demon down.

JANDAMARRA: Face the demon down.

JOE: And look where it's got me. Staring down the barrel of a gun.

JANDAMARRA *slips silently away, leaving* JOE *expecting death. When he realises no shot is coming,* JOE *almost collapses with relief. He gathers up his swag and scurries off.*

SCENE FORTY

Bush. ILAJI *stalks on, brandishing his rifle, pushing* MARRALAM *away. They are followed on by* DIBINARRA *and a* YOUNG MAN.

ILAJI: [*angrily*]   Gandayi   gilima.   **Ngalanybinggirragi yathawunggurragi milu ngayi, gima yarrangi.** [*I'm sick of it. He's always telling us to sing, he won't let us fight.*] **Blayi ngawungu dangaj'gawuwunu-ngarragi. Ngayini-ingga dangaj'gawulunu.** [***Bligh killed my father.** And now he's running around our country. I want to kill him.*] **Jandamarra-ingga wiliga.** [*Jandamarra is shielding him.*]

DIBINARRA: Ngayi   wilig.gaya.   **Nhi.ingga   malngarri   yani thatharrawurranigi.** [*He's not shielding anybody. **He's holding the whitefellers back.***]

A furious ILAJI *fires his rifle out over the audience, not noticing* JANDAMARRA *enter. He turns and sees* JANDAMARRA.

ILAJI: [*nervously*] Ngayi milay-nya— [*I didn't know you were—*]

JANDAMARRA *holds out a fist to* ILAJI. *He uncurls his hand and there is the necklace of bones.*

Nginyjaga? Ngadigaya? [*What the hell? Where did you find it?*]

JANDAMARRA *puts a finger to his lips.*

JANDAMARRA: Ngayi birrganyguwina. [*Don't even ask.*]

He puts the necklace into ILAJI's *hand.*

Wadgingira Iminyji-yawu. [*I'm going to Iminyji.*]

MARRALAM *and* ILAJI *exchange an apprehensive look.* DIBINARRA *smiles.*

Yilimbirri Unggud wabiyalhaa-ngarri. Digalarri ngarragi-ingga guda. **Mantha wadbingay-nhi. Mulngunyu wabaumi ngarragi, winyiwayi ngarragi junba.** [*Yillimbirri Unggud is sniffing the air. I*

*can feel it in my guts. **I'm going to face him. He can smell my sweat,
and hear my song.**] Marralam.way, Wangamarra, wadbirra ma?
[Marralam, Wangamarra, will you come with me?] [To DIBINARRA]*
Muwayi yarrangi gurrijbinggirragi. [To ILAJI] **Milu ngay. [Look
after our country.** [To ILAJI] **And no fighting.**]
ILAJI: Yuwai.

> DIBINARRA *blesses* JANDAMARRA, MARRALAM *and* WANGAMARRA
> *the singer in turn, with a look, a hand on the shoulder, and a quiet
> word. The three depart.* ILAJI *and* DIBINARRA *exit stage right.*

SCENE FORTY-ONE

Lights up on MINGO MICK *at Lillimooloora.* JOE *and* FORREST *enter,
arguing, followed by a* TROOPER.

JOE: It's arse about, that's what I'm telling you. I should've been asked.

FORREST: How could we, with you out scouring the wilderness for weeks
on end? They're on their way. Fifteen hundred head of prime beef
cattle.

JOE: Pigeon's still out there.

FORREST: There's been no sightings for months. He could be dead for
all we know. A spear in his belly from some jealous buck. It's now or
never, Joe. They're saying in Perth that if the Kimberley doesn't turn
round soon, they'll give up on us, and I'm not going to let that happen.

JOE: What would they know?

> FORREST *strolls over to* MINGO MICK.

FORREST: Picked up any sign?

MINGO MICK: Nothing fresh.

FORREST: You're closing in though, aren't you?

MINGO MICK: Might be.

FORREST: You'll do it, Micky, I know you will... They tell me that boy
of yours is putting on weight. He's being looked after well, I hear.

> FORREST *exits with the* TROOPER. MINGO MICK *glares at* JOE *as he
> paces past.*

JOE: What?

> JOE *looks away, then hurries off.*

JACKY *limps on, looking around to make sure all the whitefellers are gone. He is nervous, but excited.*

JACKY: **Yoo garn gidim Bijin. Ee Jalgangurru.** Mee noa jubee yor wird blu thuddun. Liegu midijin man. [*You can't catch Pigeon. He's Jalgangurru. I don't know what you call it. Like a medicine man.*]

MINGO MICK *stays silent, knowing, powerful.*

Yoo joodim guddu boolid—nujing—ee gorn. Ee jainjim lungu bird or eneejing. Ee blai uwai. [*You shoot him with a bullet—nothing— he'll be gone. He can change into a bird, or anything. He'll fly away.*]

MINGO MICK: Mudbee Jagee. [*Maybe, Jacky.*]

He reaches under his shirt and pulls out an amulet similar to Jandamarra's, on a thong around his neck. He blows gently on it.

JACKY *drops his head. He stands frozen for a moment gathering his wits, before scurrying off as fast as his bad leg will let him. But before he makes it off:*

Hey, Jacky.

JACKY *turns.*

Thurrun Mayannie weye Jandamarra gudim, ee dordu blungu yoo indid? [*Jandamarra's woman, Mayannie, she's your daughter, isn't she?*]

JACKY: [*panicky*] Yoo leebim loan! [*You leave her alone!*]

A light on MARRALAM.

MARRALAM: It took us ten days hard walking to get to Iminyji Unggud's place. I didn't go in with him. I waited nearby.

Projected animation #17: Snake, dim and thin.

JANDAMARRA *and* WANGAMARRA *climb up onto a ledge.* JANDAMARRA *does the gesture of a hand to each armpit and the tossing of a pebble.*

JANDAMARRA: Iminyji, ngayini ngindaji Jandamarra. [*Iminyji, it is me,* JANDAMARRA.]

WANGAMARRA *begins to sing.* JANDAMARRA *sits and joins him.*

MINGO MICK *becomes alert, prowling the floor, sniffing the air.*

JANDAMARRA *and* WANGAMARRA *are still singing. There is a faint tremor: Yilimbirri Unggud's noise, low but distinct.* JANDAMARRA *gets to his feet, raises a hand high.*

Projected animation #17 continues, but now the snake is bright and thin.

The noise seems to almost take on the rhythm of words, deep and indistinct.

YILIMBIRRI UNGGUD: **Ngalanyba, guju wudgawudagi. Bilirri-nhir ban.gawayali.** [*Keep singing. The bones are long gone, but the spirit can return.*]

The noise passes. JANDAMARRA *and* WANGAMARRA *join* MARRALAM *at his spot on the range.*

JANDAMARRA: **Wulaami.** [*He spoke.*]

JANDAMARRA *and* WANGAMARRA *exit.*

MARRALAM: Yilimbirri Unggud spoke to him again. I was dying to know what had been said, but I didn't dare to ask, and he hardly spoke a word to me all the way back to Yilimbirri's spring.

Transition.

SCENE FORTY-TWO

The BUNUBA *gather.* JANDAMARRA *is surprised to see* JACKY *with the others.*

JANDAMARRA: **Nginyjaga-nhi-ma?** [*What's wrong?*]
DIBINARRA: Mingo Mick.
JANDAMARRA: **Ban.garay-ma limba-yawu?** [*Is he back with the police?*]
JACKY: Limalurruyuwa yathari. **Jalgangurru nginyji-jangi.** [*He's there at Limalurru. He's a magic man, like you.*]
JANDAMARRA: **Ngayi ngayini jangi nyirraji gurama. Limba.u bulba dayga.** [*No, he's not like me. He's wearing a uniform.*]
DIBINARRA: Nginyjaga mi Iminyji yuwa? [*So what happened at Iminyji?*]
JANDAMARRA: **Wulaami...** [*He spoke...*]

A pregnant silence.

'**Ngalanyba. Guju wudgawudagi, bilirri-nhir ban.gawayali.**' [*'Keep singing. The bones are long gone, but the spirit can return.'*]

Nginyjaga-ma wilalari. **Nhir-ma bilirri? Ngarragu-ma bilirri?**
[*Touching his arm*] **Ngarragi guju burrudi gurrijgila.** [*I don't
know what he means. His spirit? My spirit? I still have my bones.*]

DIBINARRA *looks towards* YILIMBIRRI, *then back at* JANDAMARRA.

DIBINARRA: Ngayi-yarra miluwayini nganggu. **Malngarri-yarra buga.**
[*Maybe he was wasn't wild with you. Maybe it was the white boy.*]

JANDAMARRA: Nginyjaga wilalanggira? [*What are you talking about?*]

DIBINARRA: **Duluggawuwaninyi malngarri buga, nginyji gudama?**
[**When that white boy died, were you there next to him?**]

JANDAMARRA: Garuwa yuwa warayay. **Ngayini ngindaji warangay.**
[*He was at the spring. I only came this far.*]

> He realises what DIBINARRA is driving at, and looks at him,
> shocked.

Ngayi! **Linji.u bilirri? Linji.u guju?** [*No! Lindsay's spirit?
Lindsay's bones?*]

WANGAMARRA: [*sung*] Unggud bila wila, Unggud bila wila
Balara ma nginyji Balara ma nginyji

The song continues softly beneath the next scene.

SCENE FORTY-THREE

MARY *and* JOE *enter. He is organising weapons, readying to leave.*

JOE: [*tormented, defiant*] Of course he's still alive.

MARY: You've seen him, haven't you?

> JOE's *silence is all the answer she needs. She starts shaking him.*

You bastard! You cruel bastard! Tell me. Tell me!

JOE: He said he wanted to stop the fighting.

MARY: Did you talk about Lindsay?

JOE: He reckons one of them snakes Lindsay talked about lived in that
spring, where he died. He says it was the country—the power of that
snake—that killed Lindsay.

MARY: He told you this himself?

JOE: With his gun at me head. Reckoned that snake ran away cos Lindsay
buggered up its place. The land is crying, and everything is sick, he
said, since Lindsay went there.

MARY: And then he just let you go?

> JOE *looks at her, but cannot summon an answer.*

He lets you live, yet still you… you…

JOE: I've no choice. We're bound, him and me. I've got to see it through.

> *A silence, then:*

MARY: Lord have mercy on us.

> JOE *picks up a bedroll and rifle.* MARY *stands stiffly as he gently kisses her cheek, then leaves. She watches him go, lost in her thoughts, and does not see* JANDAMARRA *enter.*

JANDAMARRA: Missus Bligh, I need to talk to you.

MARY: [*whirling around*] Pigeon?… Is it you?

JANDAMARRA: It's me. Jandamarra.

MARY: [*hesitantly*] Jandamarra… You talked to Joe?

JANDAMARRA: Yes.

MARY: You told him that everything is sick since Lindsay died? That the land is crying out?

JANDAMARRA: That's right.

MARY: Crying. That's what I've been hearing. I can never tell if it's Lindsay, or the land, or just me. But that's what I've felt, since the day Joe dug up Lindsay's bones.

JANDAMARRA: [*struggling for the words*] J— Joe took his bones away?

> *She nods nervously.*

MARY: After the fight at Windjana. He took them away.

JANDAMARRA: Bilirri nganggi urugawuwila! Guju nganggi udgalha! [I will take your spirit! Your bones will be lost!] It *was* Lindsay!

MARY: What?! What are you talking about?

JANDAMARRA: That day. When Lindsay died. The rainbow snake spoke, 'I will take your spirit', he said. 'Your bones will be lost.' I thought it was me he was angry at, but it was Lindsay, not me.

MARY: Oh… my… God!

> *He takes* MARY*'s hands in his.*

JANDAMARRA: Mary… I will ask Yilimbirri Unggud to send Lindsay's spirit home.

> JANDAMARRA *leaves her, climbing the range.*

MARY: That was the last time I saw him.

SCENE FORTY-FOUR

The singing continues.

As MARRALAM *talks: we see* JACKY *running to the singers, and some leaving with him;* JANDAMARRA *taking position up high, rubbing a pebble under his armpits and tossing it;* MINGO MICK, MARY *and* JOE *each taking up separate positions on stage.* JOE *has a cross.*

MARRALAM: We kept singing, like Yilimbirri Unggud told us to. But then Jacky got word to us about the mob of cattle coming into Limalurru. He said they were going to push them through the Oscar Gap. To our side of the range. For three years we'd held them up. Jandamarra had given his word that he wouldn't let them set up any sort of station on our side of the range. Now they were coming. He said he'd keep that promise, but first he had to sing Yilimbirri Unggud home.

> MARRALAM *exits.* JANDAMARRA *spreads his arms wide as he looks to the heavens.*

JANDAMARRA: **Nginyji ban.gawirali muwayi.yawu. Garrgawu nyirraji ganday muwayi.** [*Come back home. Leave that bad place.*] **Malngarri buga bilirri banggawayali.** [*You must let go of that white boy's spirit.*] **Ngarranyi-way nganggawila.** Bilirri ban.gawayali, nginyji-ingga jimi. [*Give him to his mother. Return it, like you said to me.*] **Ban.gawirali muwayi yawu.** [*Come back home.*]

> *Projected animation #18: Snake, bright and fat, returns and breathes.*
>
> *A sound begins to build—the snake sound.* JANDAMARRA *gets to his feet, raises an arm, then another.*
>
> *The others are also on their feet, wondering, alert, sensing something.*

MARY: Lindsay?... Lindsay!

> *The sound peaks. Then subsides with a whistling, sucking tone.*

MARY *exits, smiling broadly.*

JANDAMARRA, *back turned, slowly, slowly lowers his arms.*

JOE *looks all around, wonderingly.* MINGO MICK *looks knowingly, then turns his gaze on* JOE.

MINGO MICK: You've got him inside your head now, haven't you?

JOE *turns, startled, holding the cross behind his back, as if to hide it.*

JOE: Who?

MINGO MICK: Jandamarra.

    JOE *looks away, unwilling to admit it, as* MINGO MICK *moves closer.*

You rode with Lawrence, hey?

    JOE *nods.*

Was it hell?

JOE: I didn't think so at the time.

MINGO MICK: He's holding me nephew in Roebourne Jail. Forrest's orders. If I don't get the job done up here, they reckon he'll be sent to Rottnest Island... Not many come back from there.

JOE: No choice.

MINGO MICK: No choice.

    The sounds of cattle can be heard.

He'll be in there, living inside you till the day you die.

JOE: Jandamarra.

MINGO MICK: The herd's on the move. Time to earn our keep.

    MINGO MICK *puts on his hat and strolls off.*

    JOE *stares after him. He moves over to the Lillimooloora grave and kneels. He forces the cross into place. It stands there, slightly askew.*

JOE: Lindsay... I'm sorry.

    He gets to his feet again and makes his way off.

SCENE FORTY-FIVE

DIBINARRA *joins* JANDAMARRA *at Yilimbirri, where Lindsay died. He cups his hands and takes a sip of water, testing it.*

DIBINARRA: Jala̱ngurru... **Ba̱n.garay!** [*It's good.... **He's back!**]

He places a hand on JA̱NDAMARRA's *shoulder.*

N̲ginyji.i̱ngga, manyjayima jala̱ngurru. **Muwayi gigawuni yarra̱ngi.**
[*You have done it, you've made it good!* ***The land will thrive again.***]
Junba bagaway-nhir. [***There will be songs for this.***]

WA̱NGAMARRA: [*sung*] Yalu̱nggani jawulja birrirri ̱nginba ̱ngani
              Yalu̱nggani jawulja birrirri ̱nginba ̱ngani

JA̱NDAMARRA *gives a nod of acknowledgement, then:*

JANDAMARRA: N̲gurru wadbingay. **N̲galabani milawingay.** [*I'm going.*
***I've got to join the others** at the gap.*]

He runs off, followed more slowly by DIBINARRA.

*The sound of cattle on the move, stockmen calling and cracking
whips can be heard.*

SCENE FORTY-SIX

Lights up on MARRALAM *and* BUNUBA MEN *taking up positions on the
range, as* JOE, MINGO MICK *and* TROOPERS *creep in to take up positions
below.*

MARRALAM: We waited there at the Oscar Gap.

The WARRIORS *see the approaching cattle. They manoeuvre, ready
for battle.*

Our hearts sank when we saw the dust of this huge mob of cattle coming. There were half a dozen stockmen, a mob of troopers and trackers, and Mingo Mick. And no sign of Ja̱ndamarra.

Chaos. Shouts and gunshots.

ILAJI *steps forward, crouches, fires.*

ILAJI: Yuwana! Wadbalima! [*I got him! I killed one!*]

But as he shouts, he takes a bullet himself. Another WARRIOR
darts out and drags him back, but even as he disappears, ILAJI *is
triumphant.*

[*Gasping*] **Yuwana wadbalima ̱ngawu̱ngu!** [*I got one, Dad!*]

The battle continues, with MARRALAM *shooting and ducking as he talks.*

MARRALAM: Ilaji finally got his revenge. It was the first whitefeller we killed in three years. But we couldn't hold them back. Ilaji, Rawali, Dibag—all shot.

He is the last man standing, as MINGO MICK *and* JOE *approach him from behind.*

A few got away, but Mingo got me.

MARRALAM *is disarmed and led off as* JINI *and* MAYANNIE, *heavily pregnant, enter.*

JINI: The other women took all the kids and ran for their lives. Mayannie and I had to dodge the patrols, but we managed to find Jandamarra and Dibinarra coming back from Yilimbirri and warn them.

JANDAMARRA *and* DIBINARRA *enter.*

MAYANNIE: Bujani. Milu.ngayi. [*It's finished. We can't fight any more.*] [*Moving closer to him*] Ngindaji nganggi buga. [*Your child.*]

She takes his hand and places it on her stomach.

Wadbirra winami-yawu rawurriga, ngayi diganbirrarri. [***Let's go to the hill country,** they'd never find us.*]

JANDAMARRA: **Malngarri-ingga,   bilagawirrama   yarrangi. Dangajgawunburrunugu Jambiyindi-wayi.** [*They would follow us. They would kill you. And this baby.*]

MAYANNIE: [*desperately*] **Ngayi diganbirrarri.** [*They won't find us.*]

JANDAMARRA: Ngayi ganbanya. **Ngayi garrgalu Marralam janga janga ngarri.** [*I can't come. I can't leave Marralam on the chain.*]

MAYANNIE: [*wailing*] Ngayi! [*No!*]

He holds her gently.

JANDAMARRA: Nginyji wadbira maaninga. Ngarranyi Dibinarra way. **Wadbinggirragi birriga balili-yawu. Yathawura nyirraji-yuwa buga wilharrawuni.** [*You must go tonight. With Mum and Dibinarra. Go to the limestone place. Stay there till the baby is born.*]

She shakes her head, sobbing, as he disengages and backs away.

Wadbungay yinggirranggu nyirraywa baljuwa…. Ngay.yarra. [*I'll come to you there later… If I can.*]

He turns and runs off.

JINI: That was the last time we saw him.

SCENE FORTY-SEVEN

MARRALAM *walks in the plodding* CHAIN GANG, *surrounded by* TROOPERS *and* MINGO MICK.

MARRALAM: We watched the stockmen push those cattle on through the gap. It felt like everything was over. When we started on the long walk west to Derby I thought I was leaving my country for the last time. I felt that chain cutting into my neck. Bligh didn't go with his cattle. He stuck as close to Mingo Mick as he could. We were all watching the ranges, thinking about Jandamarrra. It was near sundown on our third day when he came, running hard out of the setting sun.

> *The* CHAIN GANG *comes to a halt as* JANDAMARRA *runs in through the audience and across the stage into the bush.*

Jandamarrra had set a trap. But he didn't quite make it.

> JANDAMARRA *runs on. Just before he reaches safety he is shot. He collapses, clutching at his guts.*
>
> MINGO MICK *enters, with rifle, kneels, aims.*
>
> JOE *runs on. He stops by* MINGO MICK, *puts a hand on the rifle and pushes the barrel down.*

JOE: I should finish what I started.

> JOE *walks slowly over to* JANDAMARRA, *who is sprawled on his stomach. He pulls a revolver from his belt, closes his eyes, then kneels. He brings the gun to* JANDAMARRA*'s temple.*
>
> *Suddenly* JANDAMARRA *whirls, bringing his rifle up. The sound of simultaneous shots.* JOE *staggers backwards, shot in the hand, blood spilling. Shot yet again,* JANDAMARRA *disappears into the ranges.*

MARRALAM: At sun-up they sent one of the trackers out to get the horses. Jandamarra dropped him with a single shot, and then the bullets started flying—from all directions. [*Shaking his head*] I thought he was going to set us free. But then the firing stopped. I think Mingo must have winged him again.

The PRISONER *behind* MARRALAM *on the chain gang taps him on the shoulder and points. All the* MEN *on the chain gang look to the sky.*

Ngumurru... Winyji. [*Clouds... the rain coming.*]

JANDAMARRA'S VOICE: **Yilimbirri Unggud ban.garay!** [*Yilimbirri Unggud is back!*]

On the chain, the BUNUBA MEN *swell with pride and happiness.*

MARRALAM: [*reverently*] Yilimbirri Unggud ban.garay... That was the last time I saw him.

A TROOPER *jerks on the chain, and the* GANG*'s slow progress resumes.* MARRALAM *speaks as they exit.*

Mingo tracked Jandamarra all that day and the next, back to near Tunnel Creek. He left a blood trail like a wounded roo.

SCENE FORTY-EIGHT

MINGO MICK *enters, eyes down, following a trail. He looks up to the range.*

MINGO MICK: [*calling*] Jandamarra!

Silence.

Ie gin loogim wijai yoo bin goa. Yoo garn gidard brom deye. Or mudbee yoo gudim nuthuwun dunool, ai? Mudbee Ie torgin lungu nujing. [*I can see which way you've gone. You can't escape from there. Unless you've got another tunnel, hey? Maybe I'm talking to a ghost.*]

Another silence.

Lijin lungu mee. Bileejman gumin ub. Gilojub nu. Blie guddu orlubud doo... Ie bin fiendim yors bild guddu boolid. Yoo mudbee runard nou. [*Listen to me. The police are coming. They're close now. Bligh's there too... I found your bullet belt. You must have run out now.*]

Another silence... then:

JANDAMARRA: [*offstage*] Ie guddim wun boolid. Nub blu yoo. [*I've got one. Enough for you.*]

A horse whinnies.

MINGO MICK: [*looking off*] Thurrun dem nou. [*That's them now.*]

A shot, then JANDAMARRA *appears and shoots.*

A TROOPER *runs on with a bandaged* JOE *and* TRACKER.

TROOPER: [*as they enter*] Come on!

JANDAMARRA *fires again, aiming towards them.*

TRACKER: Shit!

TROOPER: Take cover!

They dive into shelter stage left. JINI *and* MAYANNIE *enter stage right and sit as witnesses.*

JANDAMARRA *lays down his rifle and climbs to the top ledge. When he stands tall he and* MINGO MICK *lock eyes.*

JOE *steps into view, gun at the ready, but not aimed.* MINGO MICK *stays eyes locked on* JANDAMARRA. *With one hand he signals* JOE *to stop.* JOE *accepts this, lowering his gun, and retreats.*

MINGO MICK: **Thurrun jinaig?** [***The snake?***]

JANDAMARRA: **Yilimbrri Unggud, ee bin gum bag.** [***Yilimbirri Unggud. He's come home.***]

JINI and MAYANNIE *begin singing a lament softly, beating time with clasped hands pounding their laps, which is sung under the action.*

JINI & MAYANNIE: [*together, sung*] Dirrari wala waray, winyilay, wala
      waray, minyarri
    Dirrari wala waray, winyilay, wala waray, minyarri

JANDAMARRA *smiles as he walks to the edge of the ledge.*

MINGO MICK: **Bujee, lu mie gundree, Ie wurru bin liegu yoo, biedin bor mie gundree. Bud Ie bin bolurin nuthu road.** [***Back in my country, I could have been like you, fighting for my land. But my track went a different way.***]

JANDAMARRA: I know.

JANDAMARRA *holds out his right hand.* MINGO MICK *salutes him, and nods as* JANDAMARRA *slowly raises the hand.*

Slowly, deliberately, MINGO MICK *takes aim.*

JANDAMARRA*'s right arm is flung backwards as the shot takes him in the ball of the thumb. He spins and falls.*

Lights low as the women's song swells louder.

MINGO MICK *climbs up. He removes his police jacket, then sits cross-legged at the feet of* JANDAMARRA*'s body.*

He and the women look as JANDAMARRA*'s spirit flies away.*

Projected animation #19: Jub bird flies up and disappears upwards, centre stage.

The lights fade down on JINI *and* MAYANNIE *for a final verse of the lament.*

Blackout as the lament ends.

Projected animation #20: Snake, breathing slowly. Peaceful and powerful.

Lights up.

After applause JINI *is helped up to join the* BUNUBA *on the top level.*

JINI *holds up a hand to silence the audience.*

JINI: Jandamarra died for this country, for making it strong again. We remember by our songs.

She sweeps an arm in a wide circle, to encompass all around them.

All this land, every hill, every creek, has a song. Yilimbirri Unggud's country, we call 'im Jumbururru. This is a song for that country.

WANGAMARRA *begins, and is joined by the* FULL CAST:

WANGAMARRA: [*sung*] Yilimbirri mindi barurru ngarri jarra binma
Yilimbirri mindi barurru ngarri jarra binma
Yilimbirri mindi barurru ngarri jarra binma

Bululuwa mindi barurru ngarri jarra binma
Bululuwa mindi barurru ngarri jarra binma
Bululuwa mindi barurru ngarri jarra binma

THE END

www.ingramcontent.com/pod-product-compliance
Lightning Source LLC
Chambersburg PA
CBHW041931090426
42744CB00017B/2011

9780868199733